Table Saw Projects

WITH *Ken Burton*

POPULAR WOODWORKING BOOKS
CINCINNATI, OHIO
www.popularwoodworking.com

[READ THIS IMPORTANT SAFETY NOTICE] To prevent accidents, keep safety in mind while you work. Use the safety guards installed on power equipment; they are for your protection. When working on power equipment, keep fingers away from saw blades, wear safety goggles to prevent injuries from flying wood chips and sawdust, wear headphones to protect your hearing, and consider installing a dust vacuum to reduce the amount of airborne sawdust in your woodshop. Don't wear loose clothing, such as neckties or shirts with loose sleeves, or jewelry, such as rings, necklaces or bracelets, when working on power equipment. Tie back long hair to prevent it from getting caught in your equipment. People who are sensitive to certain chemicals should check the chemical content of any product before using it. The authors and editors who compiled this book have tried to make the contents as accurate and correct as possible. Plans, illustrations, photographs and text have been carefully checked. All instructions, plans and projects should be carefully read, studied and understood before beginning construction. Due to the variability of local conditions, construction materials, skill levels, etc., neither the author nor Popular Woodworking Books assumes any responsibility for any accidents, injuries, damages or other losses incurred resulting from the material presented in this book. Prices listed for supplies and equipment were current at the time of publication and are subject to change. Glass shelving should have all edges polished and must be tempered. Untempered glass shelves may shatter and can cause serious bodily injury. Tempered shelves are very strong and if they break will crumble, minimizing personal injury.

[METRIC CONVERSION CHART]

to convert	*to*	*multiply by*
Inches	Centimeters	2.54
Centimeters	Inches	0.4
Feet	Centimeters	30.5
Centimeters	Feet	0.03
Yards	Meters	0.9
Meters	Yards	1.1

 Published by Popular Woodworking Books, an imprint of F+W Publications, Inc., 4700 East Galbraith Road, Cincinnati, Ohio, 45236. First edition.

Distributed in Canada by Fraser Direct
100 Armstrong Avenue
Georgetown, Ontario L7G 5S4
Canada

Distributed in the U.K. and Europe by David & Charles
Brunel House
Newton Abbot
Devon TQ12 4PU
England
Tel: (+44) 1626 323200
Fax: (+44) 1626 323319
E-mail: postmaster@davidandcharles.co.uk

Distributed in Australia by Capricorn Link
P.O. Box 704
Windsor, NSW 2756
Australia

Visit our Web site at www.popularwoodworking.com for information on more resources for woodworkers.

Other fine Popular Woodworking Books are available from your local bookstore or direct from the publisher.

10 09 08 07 5 4 3 2 1

Library of Congress Cataloging-in-Publication Data

Burton, Ken.
Table saw projects with Ken Burton / by Ken Burton. -- 1st ed.
p. cm.
ISBN-13: 978-1-55870-778-8 (paperback : alk. paper)
ISBN-10: 1-55870-778-6 (paperback : alk. paper)
1. Woodwork. 2. Circular saws. 3. Woodworking tools. I. Title.
TT186.B853 2006
684'.083--dc22
2006029622

ACQUISITIONS EDITOR: Jim Stack
EDITOR: Erin Nevius
DESIGNER: Brian Roeth
PRODUCTION COORDINATOR: Jennifer L. Wagner
PHOTOGRAPHER: Kenneth Burton
ILLUSTRATOR: Michael Gellatly
WORKSHOP SITE PROVIDED BY: Windy Ridge Woodworks

[DEDICATION]

For Susan, Sarah, and Emma—you're the best!

[ABOUT THE AUTHOR] Kenneth Burton has been a professional woodworker for the past 24 years. He holds a bachelor of science degree in industrial art education from Millersville Iniversity of Pennsylvania and a master of fine arts degree in woodworking and furniture design from the School for American Crafts at the Rochester Institute of Technology.

Currently Burton operates Windy Ridge Woodworks in New Tripoli, Pennsylvania, where he designs and builds original furniture, custom cabinetry and interiors. During the summer months, you can often find him teaching workshops at the Yestermorrow School in Warren Vermont, or at Peters Valley Craft Center in Layton, New Jersey.

Burton is also the department leader for the technology education program in the Boyertown Area School District, where he teaches various elective classes.

[ACKNOWLEDGEMENTS] Putting a book together takes a lot of effort from a lot of people. Thanks to my parents, Kenneth and Marjorie Burton, for their ongoing love and support, to Susan, Sarah and Emma, who again suffered as I spent many nights and weekends both in the shop and tied to the computer.

Thanks as well to Jared Haas, who once again put time in as Mr. Hands, only to be replaced by a small electronic device that allows me to take my own picture. (Jared, if it's any consolation, I call the remote "Jared" in your honor. Despite his being pushed out of the photo business, Jared put his college degree to work and served as videographer for the accompanying DVD.

As always, I recieved some great help from various people in the industry. Thanks you, Morm Hubert of LRH EnterprisesI've really come to rely in my Magic Molder. And also to Lisa Agastoni of Freud tools—your box joint cutter set is an excellent piece of engineering.

Finally, thank you Jim Stack and the rest of the crew at F+W Publications. I really appreciate the opportunity you've provided and efforts you've put in to make this book a reality.

[TABLE OF CONTENTS]

[INTRODUCTION]

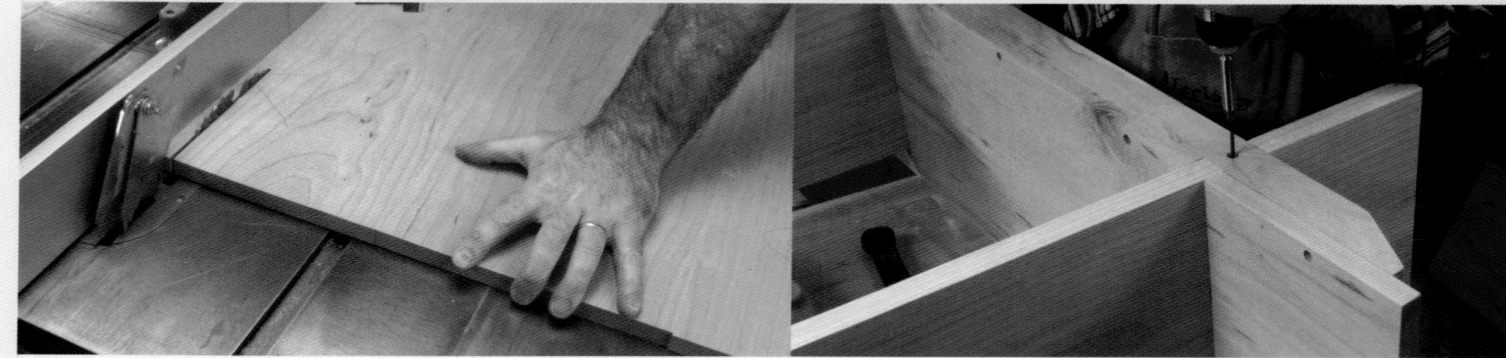

In my mind, the table saw is the heart of the woodshop. Nearly every piece of wood I use passes over its cast iron surface at least once and often many times. The saw takes rough stock, cuts it to a more manageable size and then cuts it to final size. It cuts joints and can make profiles. In short, there is little you cannot accomplish with a table saw. But what if it were the only power tool you had access to?

I started with that scary premise as I sat down to design the projects in this book. I have a shop with a complete array of tools (you'll probably see some of them in the photos), but what I tried to do was pretend that these other tools did not exist. From the beginning, I realized I would have to compromise a little here and there (table saws just don't drill holes) and that there would be some operations where I might need to use a router (mortising, for example). But I was pleasantly surprised to find that limiting myself to the table saw was really no limitation at all.

In fact, as I began building these projects, I kept coming up with new things the table saw could do (new to me, at least) and new techniques I wanted to try. I discovered I could cut mortises with the saw. (Routing them is still faster, but it is nice to know you don't have to own a plunge router). I was amazed at how good a circle a table saw can cut and how quickly. This subject came up at a talk I gave to the Lehigh Valley Woodworkers Guild. I was showing photos of the Cylindrical Chest of Drawers and the question was asked: "Would you still cut the disks with your saw if you weren't doing it for the book?" The answer is yes, I would. While you can use a router to get the same result, I have come to the

opinion that the table saw is actually faster and the final product of equal quality, so I've added the technique to my bag of tricks.

As for the projects themselves, I had several goals in mind as I designed each one. Obviously, I wanted to be able to do as much as possible on the table saw. But I didn't want the finished products to look like typical table saw projects—straight lines and square corners with a few dadoes thrown in for good measure. I wanted these things to be good-looking items that you would want to have in your house. I also wanted people to look at them and say "You used only the table saw? You must be joking!" Judging from reactions so far, I think I have accomplished this.

I hope you have fun building the projects in this book. Having built every one of them myself, I know they all work and that the drawings reflect the pieces in the photos. However, feel free to modify the plans as you see fit. I tried to make the instructions as detailed as I could within the space I had. At the start, I decided not to shown many of the mundane tasks common to every project—cutting pieces to size, etc. Rather, I tried to show the more complicated aspects of each. Please don't hesitate to contact me if you run into trouble or have suggestions for improvement.

Ken Burton

[WINDY RIDGE WOODWORKS 2006]

TRIVETS [1]

If you're looking for a quick project with a little pizzazz, consider building a trivet. The ones you find here definitely fall under the category of "scrap box projects" because they use a minimal amount of material—the kind of pieces you're likely to find in your scrap box. They make nice presents or, if you sell your work, excellent "entry-level" products you can offer at a modest price point.

If you want to share your love of woodworking with a youngster, these are great projects to build together (you cut, they can help sand, glue and clamp). In fact, my mother still has the trivet I made with help from my father—I was probably seven or eight years old at the time. I seem to recall having grand plans for making a zillion of them and selling them door-to-door, but that's another story.

Design-wise, the sky is the limit. You can follow the plans shown here or take the basic idea and put your own slant on it. Of the three designs in the photo, the circular one and the rectangular one are simple to make and follow essentially the same process. The diamond design is a little more involved, but the general idea is similar to the other two. The basic plan calls for two runners dadoed into a series of cross pieces. If you keep this plan in mind, there is no end to the possibilities.

The one problem I've come across when making a batch of trivets occurs during finishing. Each has a lot of nooks and crannies to deal with, so applying finish can be a tedious job. Spraying is one option. Or, if you prefer a wiped on finish, consider pouring the finish into a shallow tray and dipping the pieces. Then set up a rack so the excess can drain back into the tray. That's how I finished these trivets.

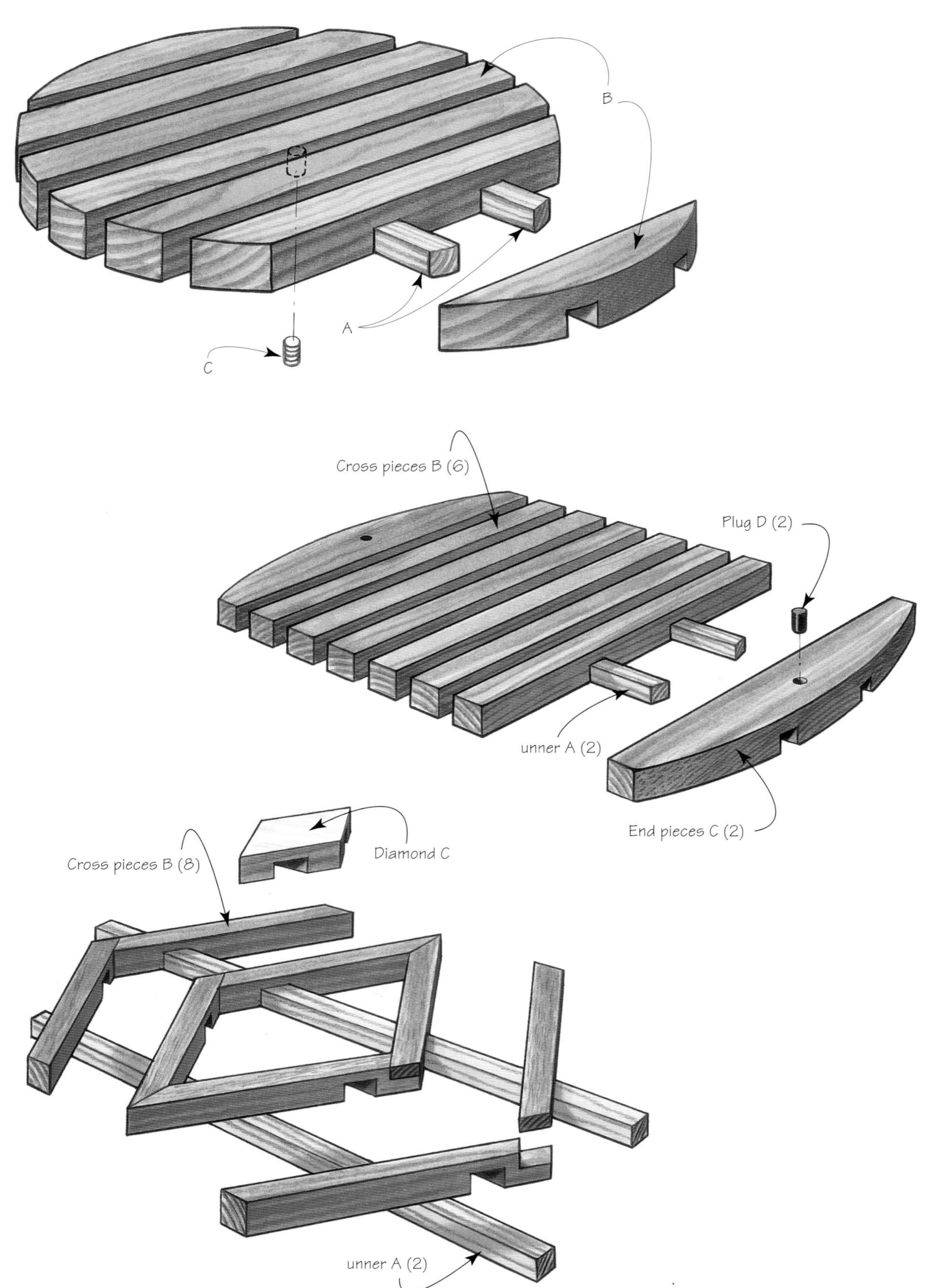
B
A
C
Cross pieces B (6)
Plug D (2)
unner A (2)
End pieces C (2)
Diamond C
Cross pieces B (8)
unner A (2)

[ROUND] inches (millimeters)

REFERENCE	QUANTITY	PART	STOCK	THICKNESS	(mm)	WIDTH	(mm)	LENGTH	(mm)	COMMENTS
A	2	runners	hardwood	1/2	(13)	1/2	(13)	9 1/2	(24)	
B	7	cross pieces	hardwood	7/8	(22)	7/8	(22)	9	(229)	
C	1	plug	hardwood						(6)	1/4" (6mm) diameter

[RECTANGULAR]

REFERENCE	QUANTITY	PART	STOCK	THICKNESS	(mm)	WIDTH	(mm)	LENGTH	(mm)	COMMENTS
A	2	runners	hardwood	1/2	(13)	1/2	(13)	12 1/4	(311)	
B	6	cross pieces	hardwood	7/8	(22)	7/8	(22)	9	(229)	
C	2	end pieces	hardwood	7/8	(22)	1 1/2	(33)	9	(229)	
D	2	plugs	hardwood							1/4" (6mm) diameter

[DIAMOND]

REFERENCE	QUANTITY	PART	STOCK	THICKNESS	(mm)	WIDTH	(mm)	LENGTH	(mm)	COMMENTS
A	2	runners	hardwood	7/16	(11)	1/2	(13)	10	(254)	
B	8	cross pieces	hardwood	3/4	(19)	1/2	(13)	6	(152)	
C	1	diamond	hardwood	3/4	(19)	2 3/8	(60)	4	(102)	

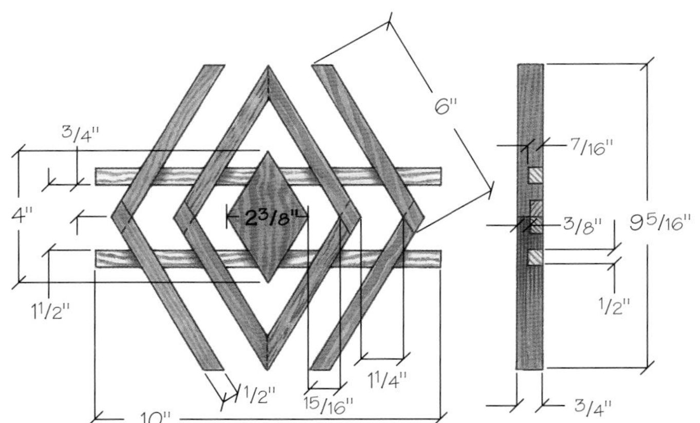

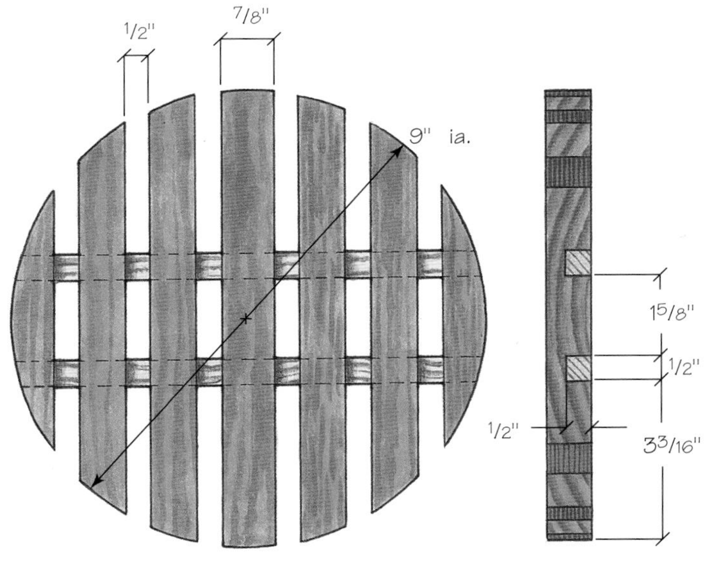

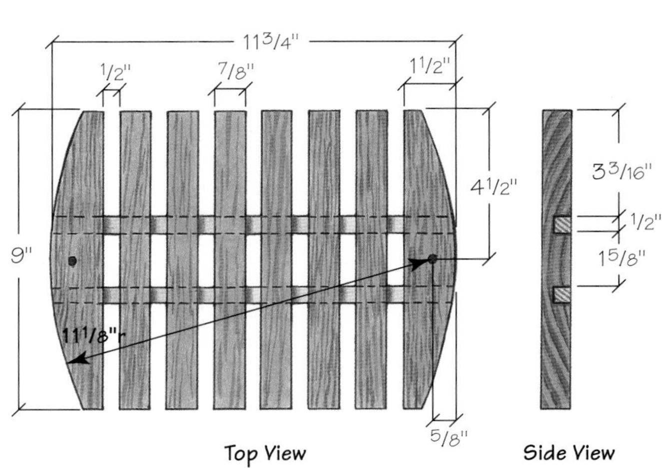

[ROUND AND RECTANGULAR]

[1] RIP THE RUNNERS

Rip the runners to the listed thickness and width. Be sure to use a push stick to keep your fingers away from the blade. Note: The piece in the photo is a scrap leftover from another project that happened to have a bull-nose profile cut on one edge. There is no need for you to duplicate this.

[2] CUT THE DADO

For the cross pieces, cut a piece to the listed thickness and length but leave it wide enough to make some, if not all, the pieces you need. Set up a 1/2" (13mm) wide dado blade and adjust its height to 1/2" (13mm). Cut two dadoes across the piece, using the miter gauge to guide the piece through the cut. Set up a stop to control the location of the dadoes.

[3] RIP THE PIECES TO WIDTH

Rip cross pieces to width. Again, use a push stick to keep your fingers at a safe distance.

[4] PUT THE CROSS PIECES ON THE RUNNERS

Apply glue to the inside of the dado cuts. Put the cross pieces on the runners, using scraps of runner as spacers. Clamp the pieces together, using two extra runners under the clamp blocks to focus the pressure where it needs to go.

[5] MEASURE TO SET UP THE JIG

Cut the curves on the trivets with the aid of a circle-cutting jig (see page 103). To set the jig for the proper radius, place it on the saw and measure out from the blade. Mark the jig, then loosen the pin and move it to align with the mark. For most cuts, the exact setting isn't critical—as long as you're within 1/8" (3mm) or so, everything will be fine.

[6] CUT THE RECTANGULAR TRIVET

Drill two 1/4-inch (6mm) holes, one in each of the wide end pieces. I drilled the holes in the top side, but they could easily go in the bottom. Make the holes about 3/8-inch (9mm) deep. Set up the jig to cut an 11 1/8-inch (282mm) radius. Place the trivet blank on the pin and cut the curve on one end by making a series of cuts, pivoting the piece slightly after each. Keep a tight grip on the piece to prevent it from spinning. Repeat the process with the second end. Plug the holes with contrasting hardwood.

[7] CUT THE ROUND TRIVET

With the round trivet, drill the 1/4" (6mm) pivot hole in the center of the middle cross piece. Set up the circle-cutting jig for a 4 1/2" (114mm) radius circle. Place the trivet blank on the pin. Achieve a round shape by making a series of cuts, turning the blank slightly after each. Again, keep a firm grip on the piece to prevent it from spinning under pressure from the blade. Sand and finish as desired.

[DIAMOND]

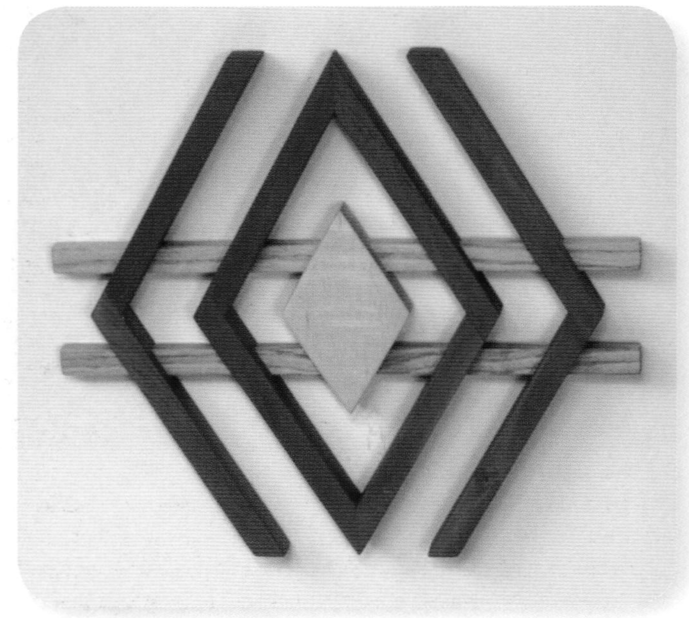

[1] CUT THE CROSS PIECES AT AN ANGLE

Cut the runners and cross pieces to the sizes listed in the materials list. Cut the ends of the cross pieces at a 60° angle. Guide the pieces through the cut with a miter gauge, using a stop to control their length.

[2] CUT THE NOTCHES

Keep the miter gauge set at 60°. Set up a 1/2"-wide (13mm) dado blade and set its depth for half the thickness of your stock. Clamp a sacrificial fence that extends past the blade to your miter gauge. This provides extra support for the pieces as well as helping to prevent tear-out. Cut a 1/2"-wide (13mm) notch on one end of each cross piece, using a stop to maintain consistency.

[3] CLAMP THE PIECES

Apply glue to the mating surfaces and clamp pairs of the cross pieces together. When the glue dries, sand everything flush.

[4] MARK A CRADLE

Cut two pieces of $^{3}/_{4}$" (19mm) plywood or MDF to serve as cradle boards. Hold one of the V-shaped pieces on top of the cradle with the V's outside corners aligned with the long edge of the cradle. Trace the V with a pencil.

[5] CUT THE CRADLE

Extend one of the layout lines all the way across the face of the cradle board. Draw square lines down the edges of the cradle from either end of the extended layout line. Place the cradle on a carrier board with the extended layout line aligned with the edge of the carrier. Adjust the rip fence so the saw cuts along the edge of the carrier. Screw fences to the carrier to hold the cradle in position. Add a toggle clamp to the carrier to help hold the piece in position. Clamp the cradle in place and guide the carrier along the rip fence to make the cut. Stop cutting at the intersection (but don't worry if you overcut the corner a little.) Carefully back the carrier out of the cut. Turn the piece over to make the second cut. Repeat the process to make a second cradle.

[6] MITER A V

Adjust the rip fence so the saw cuts right along the edge of one of the cradle boards. Hold one of the Vs in the cradle and push the cradle along the fence to miter both ends. Repeat the process with a second V.

[7] CUT THE EARS OFF THE CRADLE

While it was easier to make the layout with the V-shaped piece at the edge of the cradle, you'll need to cut the corners off the cradle so they won't interfere with subsequent operations. Set the rip fence to cut about $^{1}/_{4}$" (6mm) off the cradle boards. Note: Both cradle boards in the photo are missing their outside corners. This is not important at all—I just used some scrap.

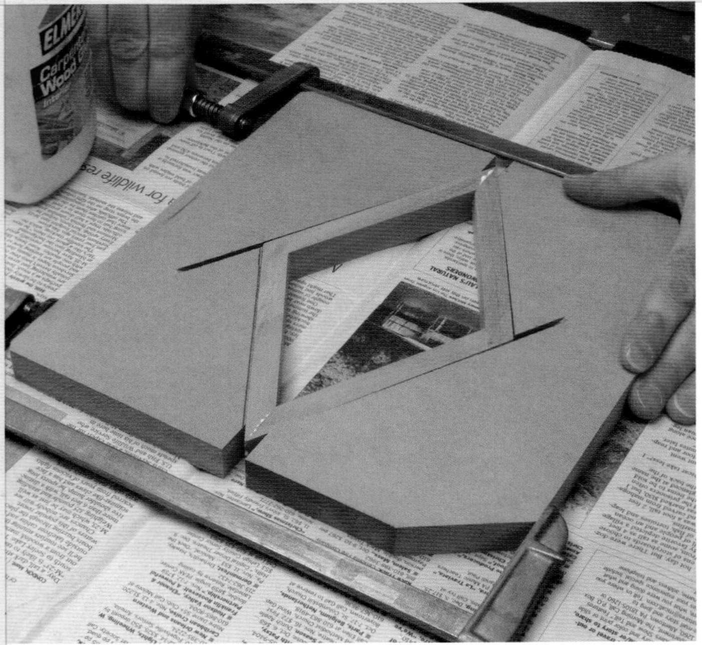

[8] GLUE THE MITERED SURFACES

Apply glue to the mitered surfaces of the two Vs you cut. Clamp the pieces together, using the cradles to help distribute the pressure. Note: Be gentle with the clamp pressure—you can easily break the pieces or, if you really crank down on the clamps, pop the corner joint.

[9] CUT THE DIAMOND

Cut the blank for the diamond to the size listed in the materials list. Lay out the diamond and place it on a carrier board with one of the layout lines aligned with the edge of the carrier. Screw fences to the carrier to hold the piece in position and add a toggle clamp for support. Set the rip fence so the saw will cut along the edge of the carrier. Guide the carrier along the fence to make the cut.

Getting Things to Line Up

Why bother to use multiple stops to cut the dadoes? It's tempting to make a single setup and simply reverse the pieces in the cradle to make the cuts. However, if any of the angles are off, the dadoes won't line up and assembly will be a real headache. If you invest a little time in the initial setup, glue-up will be much less stressful.

[10] CUT THE SECOND SIDE OF THE DIAMOND

Turn the blank over and clamp it to the carrier to make the second cut.

[11] MAKE THE THIRD CUT

Reposition the fences on the carrier board to set up for the third and fourth cuts. Make the third cut, then turn the piece over and do the fourth.

[12] CUT THE DADOES

Set up a ½"-wide (13mm) dado blade and set its height to ½" (13mm). Screw an extension fence that extends past the blade to your miter gauge. Hold one of the cradles against the fence and position stops on either side of the blade to control the location of the dadoes. Stack one of the separate Vs and the diamond in the cradle and cut the two dadoes—the first with the cradle against one stop, the second with the cradle against the second stop.

[13] CUT THE DIAMOND FRAME AND THE SECOND V

Using the same cradle and stops, load the diamond frame and the second V in the cradle, and make the dadoes. Push the pieces through the cut slowly to minimize tear-out. Glue the various cross pieces and the diamond to the runners, taking care to get the spacing right. Finish the trivet with your favorite wood finish.

CUTTING BOARDS [2]

Cutting boards might not be the most glamorous of woodworking projects, but they are not without merit. They don't use up a lot of material, and so are nice to give away as casual gifts or even as seasonal promotions for your valued customers. They are a great way to use up scraps that are too small to use, but are too big to throw away. (Don't laugh—you know exactly what I'm talking about.) And if you sell your work at craft fairs, you can usually keep the price point down to where it is manageable for most people.

Design-wise, almost anything goes. A cutting board's function is pretty much built right in, so your primary concerns are aesthetic ones. You can easily cut and sand a pretty piece of wood and call it a cutting board, or glue several contrasting pieces together for a more striking effect (Goodness knows I've made more than my share of cutting boards this way.) If you're looking to make something a little more unusual, try one of the cutting boards shown here.

The shape of the first cutting board is what I've come to call a "squircle" or square circle. It starts out as three separate pieces of wood edge glued together. The squircular cutting boards in the photo are made from oak and walnut with a $^{3}/_{16}$-inch strip of cherry glued in between. (The cherry strip doesn't show much in the photos, but it should provide a nice contrast in between the oak and the walnut as it darkens over time. The circular cutting board is made from cherry and hickory and is glued up a few pieces at a time. I usually try to use 5/4 or even 6/4 stock for cutting boards as I like the look and feel of the extra thickness. I also think thicker cutting boards are less likely to warp.

[SQUARE/CIRCLE CUTTING BOARD] inches (millimeters)

REFERENCE	QUANTITY	PART	STOCK	THICKNESS	(mm)	WIDTH	(mm)	LENGTH	(mm)	COMMENTS
A	1	side 1	hardwood	1^1⁄8	(28)	5^3⁄4	(146)	35	(889)	
B	1	side 2	hardwood	1^1⁄8	(28)	5^3⁄4	(146)	35	(889)	contrasting color to side 1
C	1	middle strip	hardwood	^{3}⁄16	(5)	1^1⁄8	(28)	35	(889)	contrasting color to both sides 1 and 2

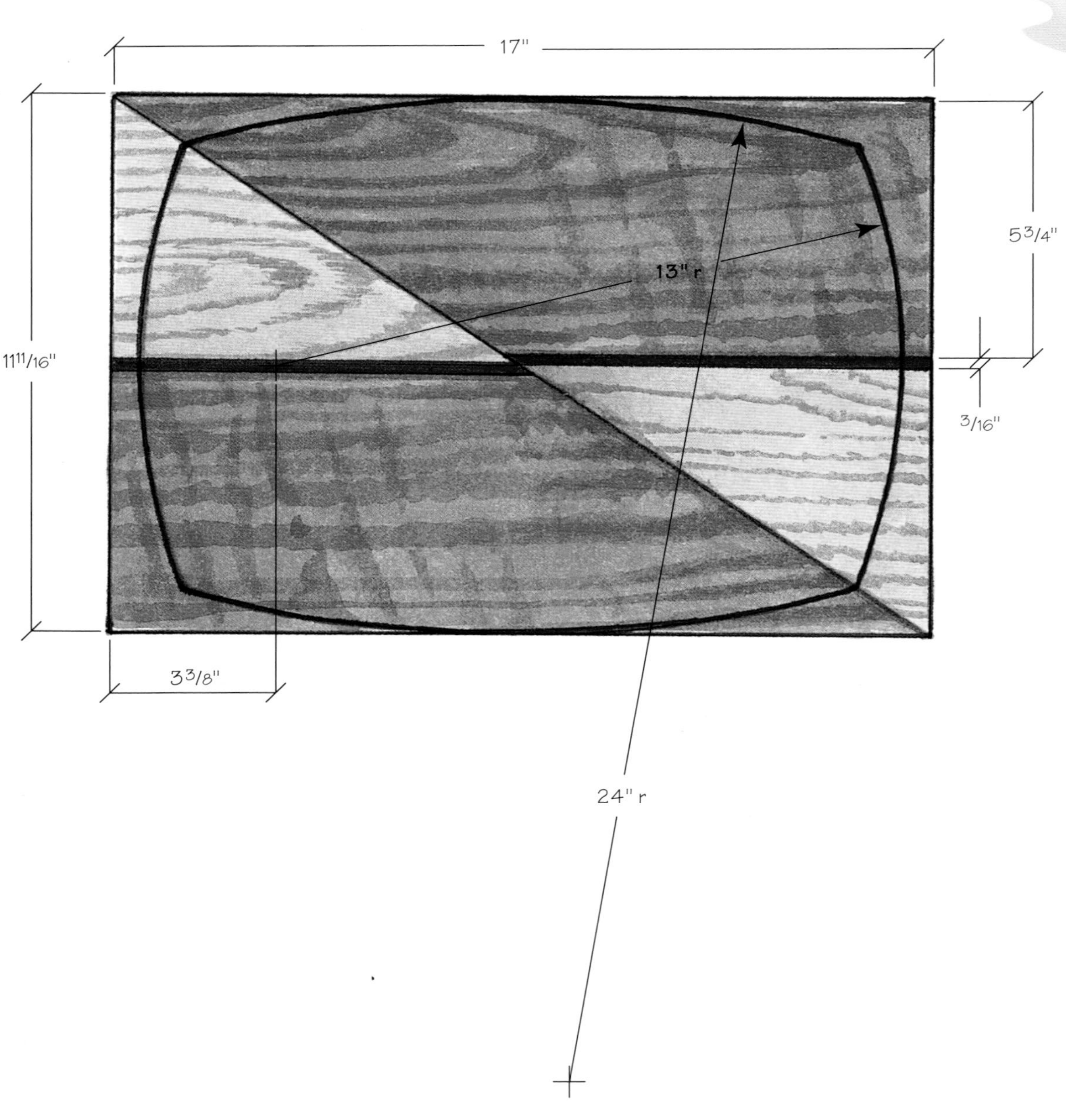

[1] CROSSCUT THE INITIAL GLUE-UP

Start by edge-gluing the three pieces of wood. In order to achieve the look here, you actually need enough material to make two cutting boards—they'll end up as color opposites of one another. Cut the glued up plank into two pieces, each 17"-long (432mm) in place after cutting the dadoes for the bottom and shelf.) Crosscut the sides to length.

[2] TRACE THE BLANK TO MAKE A CRADLE

Place one of the blanks on a piece of MDF or plywood with two of the blank's opposing corners aligned with one edge of the sheet. Trace the corner of the blank. Cut along these lines to make a cradle for both cutting and gluing the pieces. To make the cuts, measure the angles with a T-bevel. Pivot the miter gauge to the appropriate setting and guide the piece through the cuts on the table saw. Don't worry about overcutting the corner by a little to make sure the cuts meet. Make a second cradle while you're at it.

[3] CUT THE DIAGONAL

Hold the blank in the cradle and adjust the rip fence so the blade starts cutting right through the blank's corner. Guide the cradle along the fence to make the diagonal cut. Cut both blanks in this manner.

[4] GLUE UP

Run the cradle pieces through the saw, cutting the corners back $^1/_2$-inch (13mm) or so. This will keep the corners from running into each other during glue-up. Take the matching pieces from the two blanks and glue them together along the diagonal. The cradles serve to keep the clamp pressure perpendicular to the glue line. Be careful to align the pieces just right. You have two options here: You can align the tips of the triangles, or you can align the narrow strip on each piece so it looks continuous.

[5] **LAY OUT THE ARCS**

When the glue dries, unclamp the pieces and scrape away any squeeze-out. Draw center lines both along the length of the piece and across its width. Lay out the arcs; for the side arcs, the center is actually off the piece itself. To lay these out, draw a line on your bench and align the cutting board with its center line right on top of the bench line. Swing the arc with a set of trammel points or with a pencil tied to a string.

[6] **SCREW THE CARRIER IN PLACE**

Draw a center line along the length of a scrap of plywood. Align the center line on the cutting board with the center line on the plywood and some double-sided tape in between. Flip the sandwich over and screw the plywood to the cutting board. Note: I thought this would be a simple matter of driving the screws into the waste area. This worked great for the first cut, but the waste was gone when I went to set up the second cut. I ended up driving the screws through the plywood into the cutting board along the center line. I tried to space them an equal distance in from either edge. Afterwards I plugged the holes with a contrasting wood.

[7] **CUT THE SIDE ARCS**

Measure 24" (61cm) from the arc drawn on the cutting board and drill a 1/4" (6mm) hole through the plywood on its center line. Adjust the center pin on the circle-cutting sled (see page 103) so it is centered 24" (61cm) from the blade. Place the plywood on the pin and cut the arc. Note: To cut an arc on the table saw, hold the workpiece in one position and slide the sled through the cut. Then reposition the workpiece slightly and make a second cut and so on, gradually creating the arc. Repeat the process to cut the second side.

[8] **CUT THE END ARCS**

Drill 1/4" (6mm) holes for the end arcs. Adjust the circle-cutting sled to cut a 13" (33cm) radius arc. Cut the end arcs the same way you cut the side arcs.

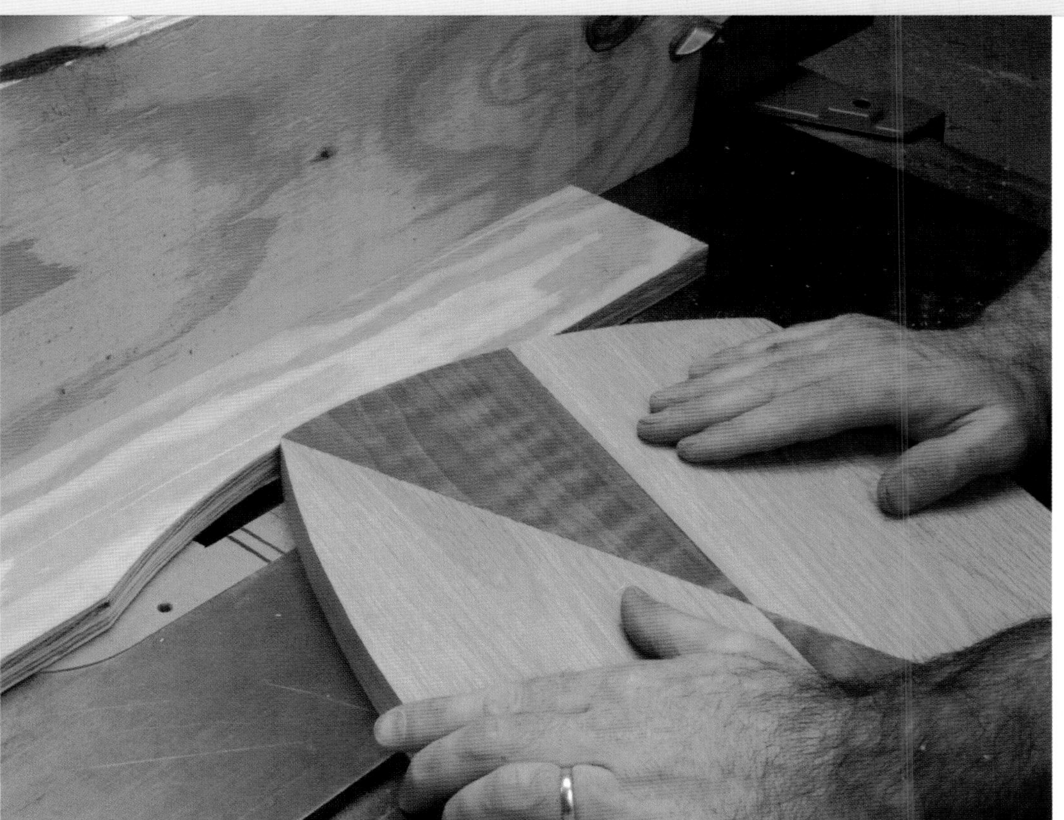

[9] CUT THE PROFILE

Chamfer the edges of the cutting board with a V-cutter in a molding head. To accommodate the curves, make two curved fences radii that match that of the two arcs. Unfortunately you'll need to cut these fences with something other than the table saw—a band saw or saber saw will work, or use a coping saw and make the cut by hand. Smooth away any lumps with sandpaper. Make the fences from ³⁄₄" (19mm) plywood or MDF, and screw them to second pieces of scrap. Lay out the curves by tracing the arcs. To use a curved fence, clamp it to the regular rip fence. Adjust the fence until the tip of the cutter comes up about ¹⁄₁₆" (1mm) behind the fence's curved face. Play with the height of the cutter to get the profile you're after. Make the cut by pushing the piece along the curve.

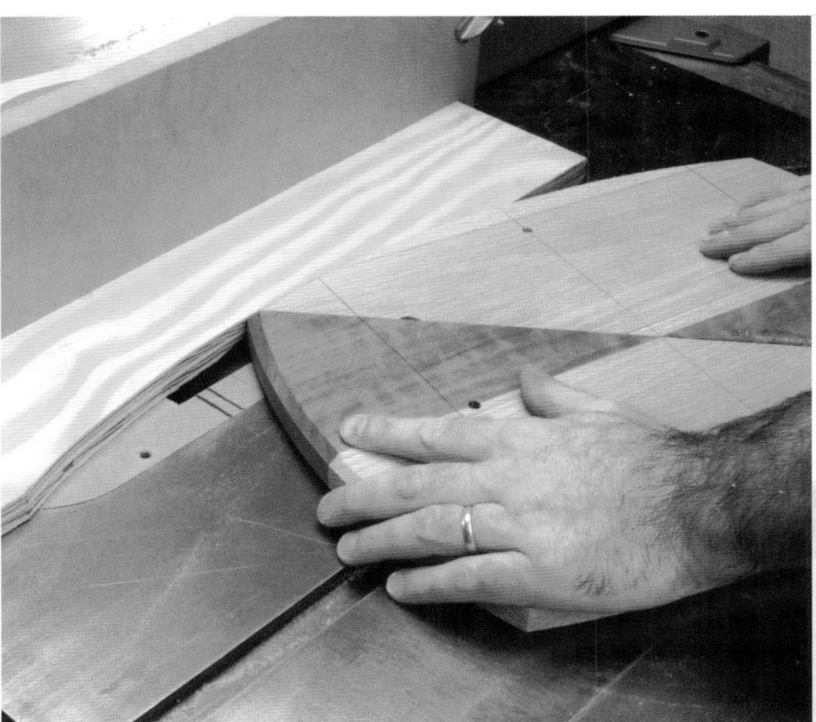

[10] CUT THE SIDES

To help eliminate tear-out, make the cuts across the ends first, then switch fences and cut along the sides. After cutting the chamfers, sand the cutting board and finish it. Once it cures thoroughly (usually after a week or so) all the solvents will have evaporated leaving behind a food-safe finish. You can also use mineral oil.

Which Glue to Use?

When choosing a glue to use for a cutting board, you need to consider that the board frequently will be immersed in water. That said, I have a cutting board I made almost twenty years ago that has stood up to years of hot dish water and even the occasional ride through the dish washer, and it was put together with regular yellow glue. However, to be on the safe side, these days I use glue that is designed for water resistance. Most frequently I use outdoor yellow glue. I have also had luck with polyurethane glue and plastic resin glue.

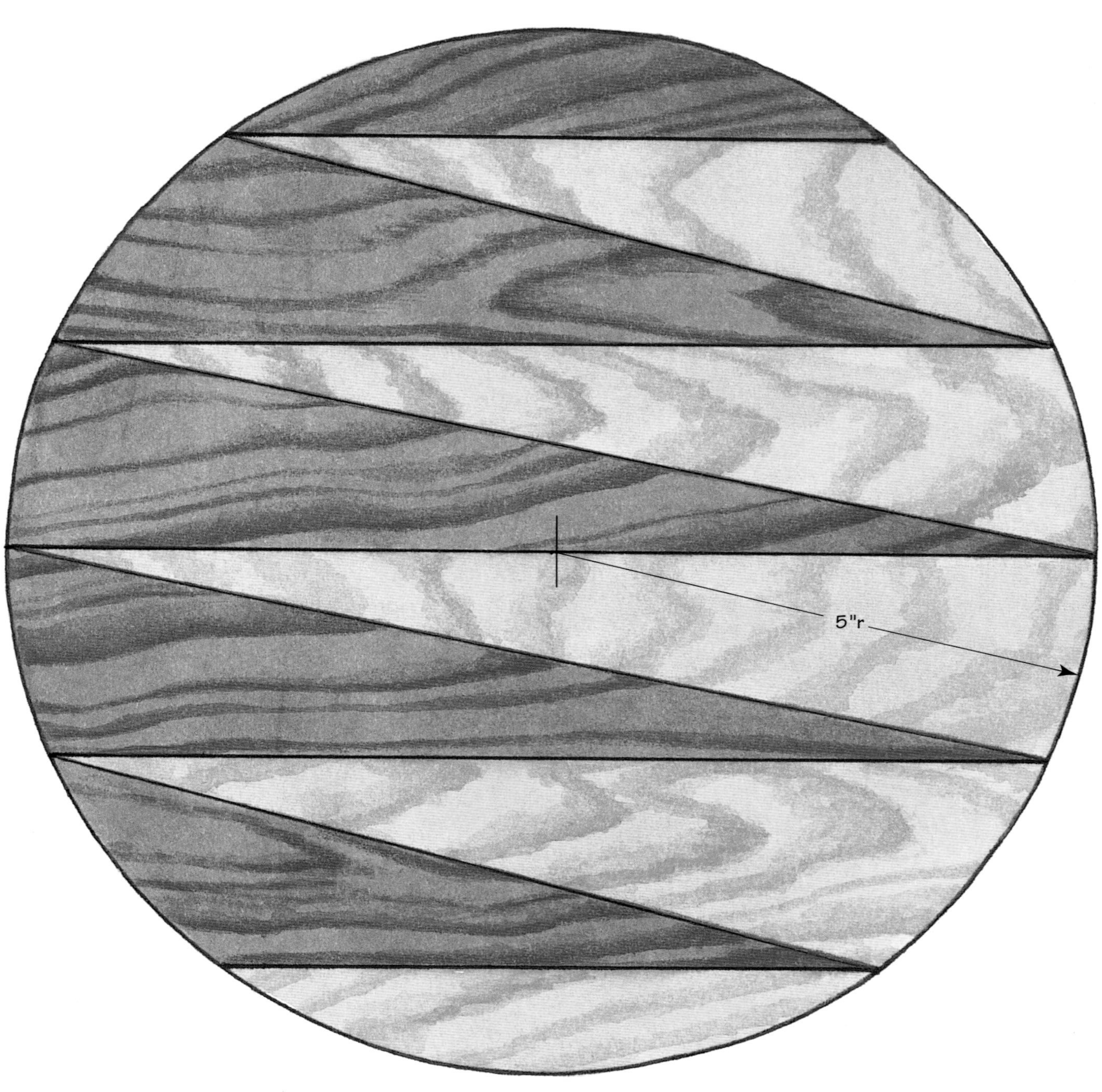
5"r

[CIRCLE CUTTING BOARD] inches (millimeters)

REFERENCE	QUANTITY	PART	STOCK	THICKNESS	(mm)	WIDTH	(mm)	LENGTH	(mm)	COMMENTS
A	2	center pieces	hardwood	1¼	(32)	2⅛	(54)	22	(559)	one of each species
B	4	outer pieces	hardwood	1¼	(32)	2	(51)	10⅝	(207)	two of each species
C	2	outside pieces	hardwood	1¼	(32)	1⅛	(28)	9⅝	(244)	one of each species

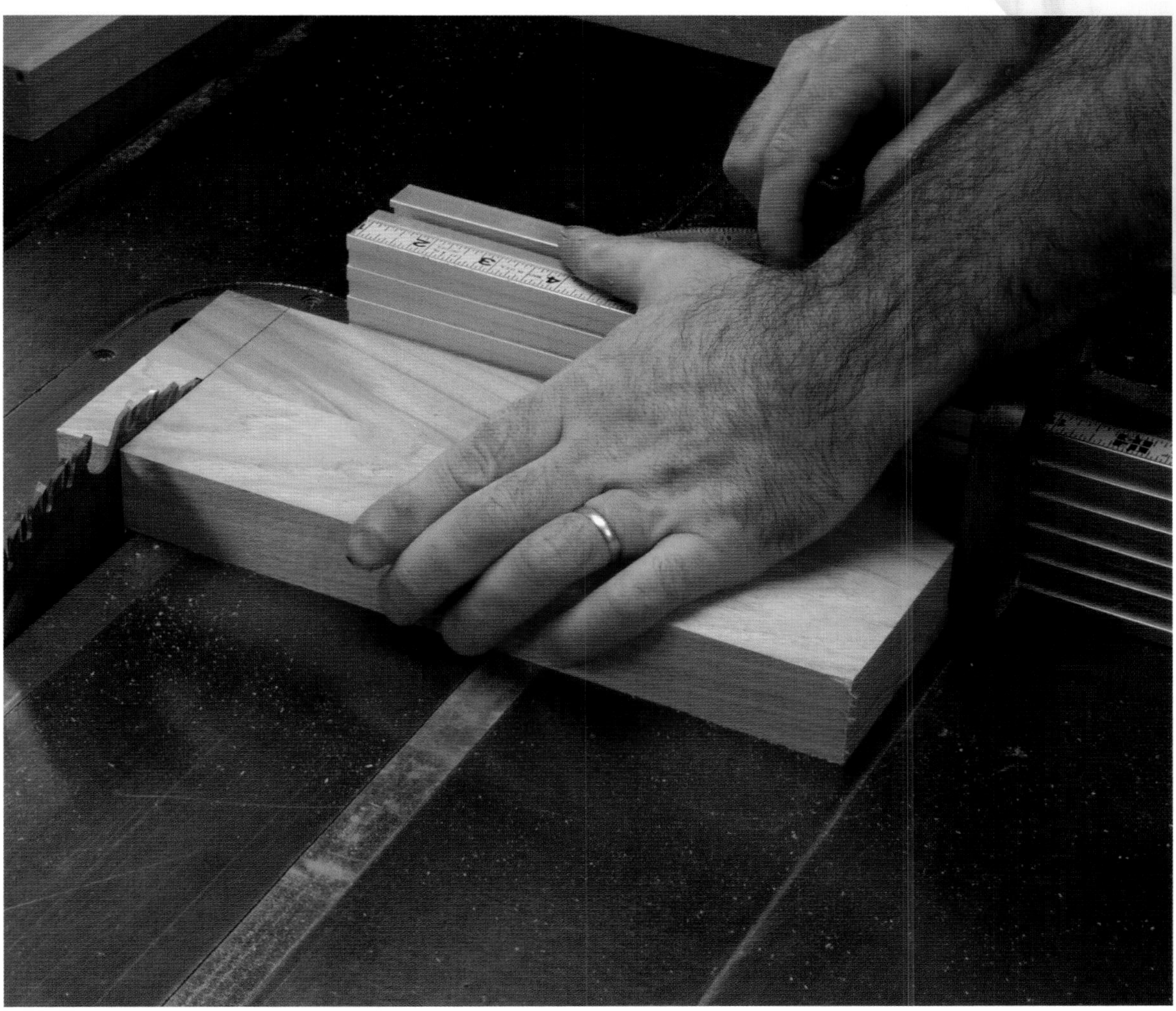

[1] CUT THE BLANKS TO LENGTH

Cut two pieces of contrasting species of wood, each 2⅛" (54mm) wide and about 22" (56cm) long. Edge-glue the pieces together. When the glue dries, crosscut the blank into two pieces 10$^{5}/_{16}$" (26cm) long.

[2] TAPER THE FIRST PIECE

Lay out a taper cut on one of the pieces. Position the piece on a carrier board with the taper layout aligned with the edge of the board. Screw fences to the carrier to hold the piece in position. Adjust the rip fence so that the blade runs along the edge of the carrier. Hold the piece in place and guide the carrier along the fence to make the cut. Cut the second piece with the same setup. This time however, cut the taper on the second species. Mark the tapered sides.

[3] RIP THE SECOND SIDE PARALLEL TO THE FIRST

Set the rip fence to make a 2"-wide (5cm) cut. Cut the pieces, running the marked sides against the fence.

[4] GLUE-UP

Glue the two pieces together along the marked sides, carefully aligning the ends. While you are gluing, also glue two additional 2"-wide (5cm) pieces to the outside of the assembly. Remember to alternate the two species.

[5] LAY OUT THE NEXT TAPERED CUT

Measure along the center glue line to find the center of the blank. Lay out a 10" (25cm) diameter circle from this point. Lay out tapers across the outer pieces. One end of the taper should occur where the circle intersects with the outer edge of the piece and the other end should occur where the circle intersects the inner (glued) edge.

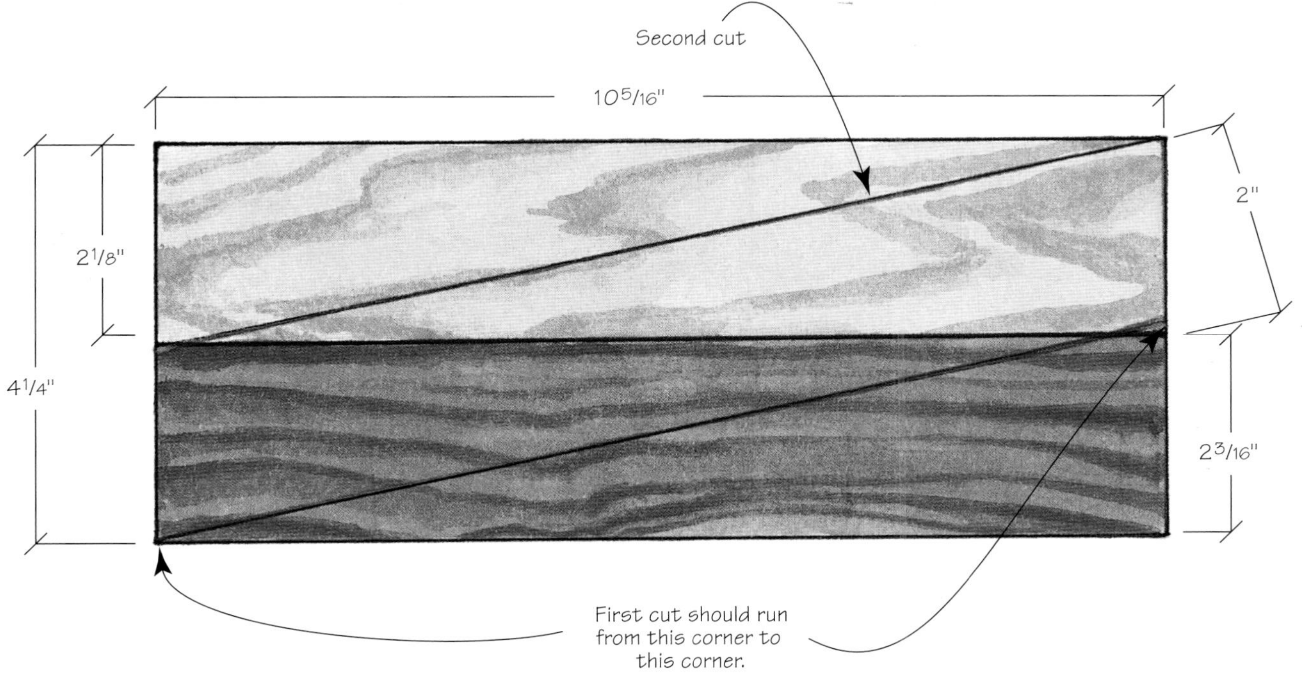

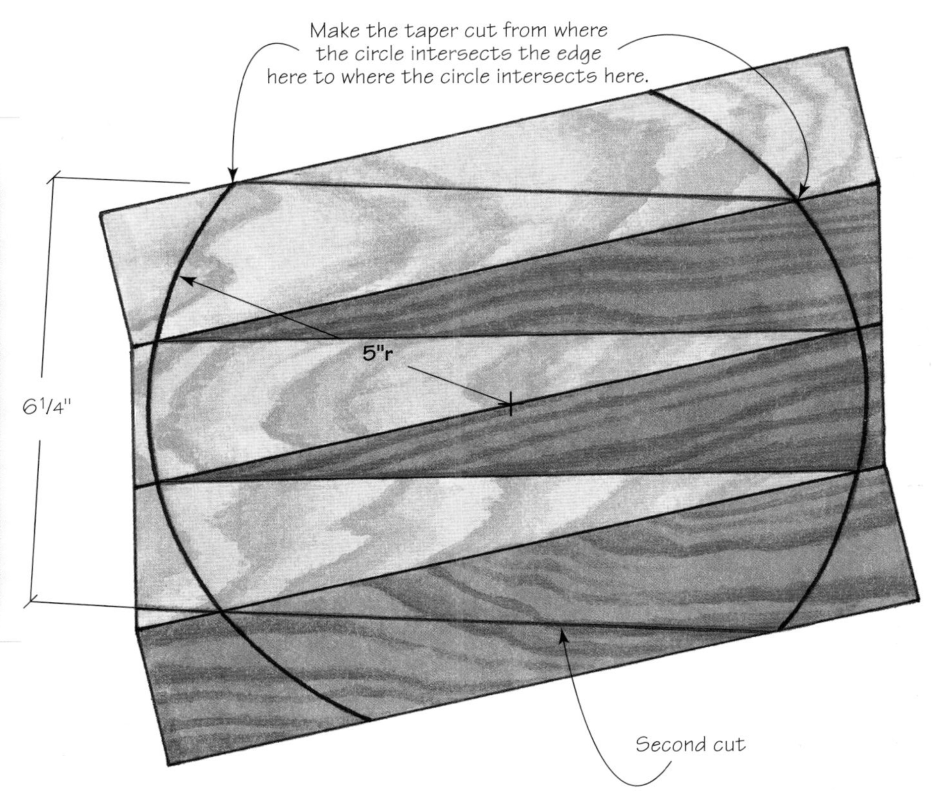

Protecting Your Bench

When I do a glue up on my bench, I try to remember to protect the bench top with some newspaper or waxed paper. This helps keep the mess to a minimum, plus it prevents the piece from actually sticking right to the bench.

[6] CUT THE NEW TAPER

Place the blank on a carrier board with this new taper layout aligned with the edge of the carrier. Screw fences to the carrier to hold the piece in position. Adjust the rip fence so the blade runs right along the edge of the carrier. Hold the piece in place and guide the carrier along the fence to make the cut as you did in step two.

[7] RIP THE SECOND SIDE

Set the rip fence to cut the second side. It should be a 6¼"-wide (16cm) cut, but cut to your layout line rather than arbitrarily setting the saw for 6¼" (16cm). Glue a second set of pieces to the outside edge of the blank. Continue the circle layout and taper these two pieces. Add two final pieces to the outside edges. These two pieces have to be only 1⅛" (27mm) wide.

[8] CUT THE BLANK ROUND

Drill a ¼" (6mm) hole at the center of the circle. Set up the circle-cutting sled (see page 103) to cut a 10" (25cm) diameter [5" (13cm) radius] circle. Place the cutting board on the pin and make repeated cuts to make the cutting board round. Sand away any facets that are left when you are through cutting.

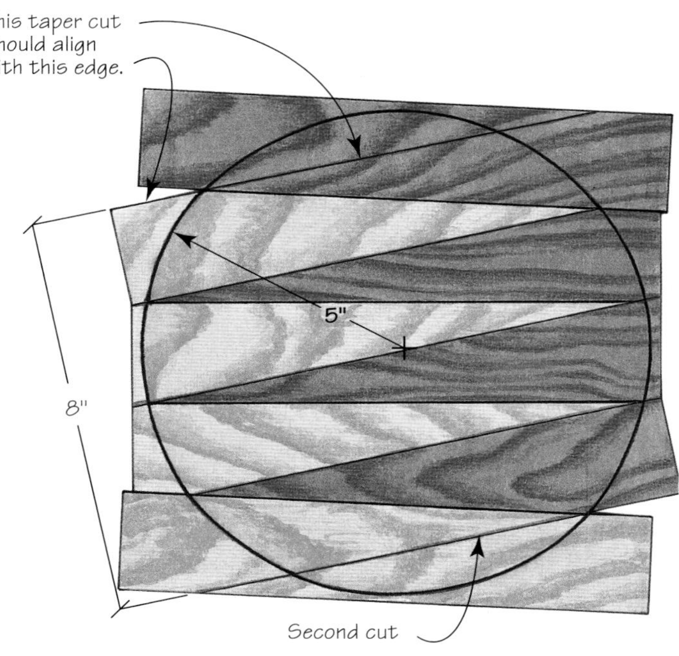

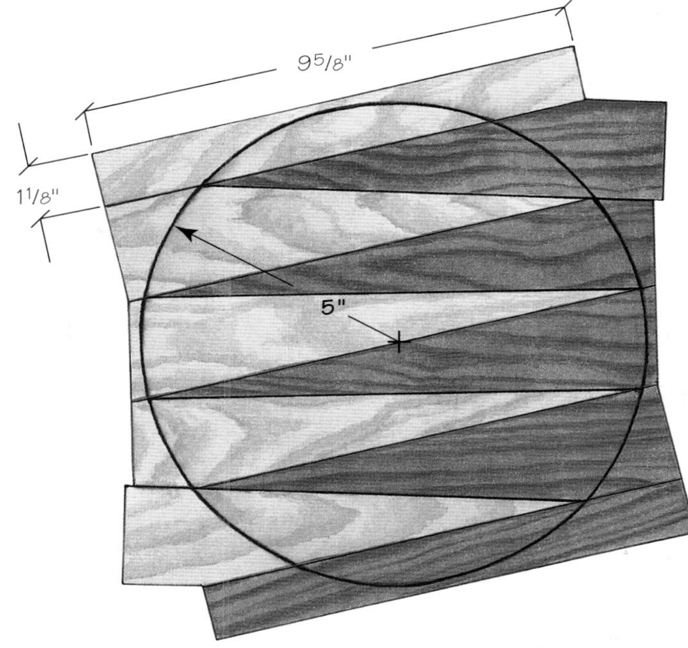

[9] PREPARING TO CUT THE PROFILE

The top edge of the cutting board is chamfered, while the bottom edge is coved. Set up a molding head with the appropriate cutter and make a concave fence with a 10" (25cm) diameter curve. Lower the molding head beneath the surface of the table. Position the fence so that the center part of the curve is over the center of the cutter and clamp it in place. Turn on the saw and slowly raise the molding head to expose as much of the cutter as you need. To get the cut started, hold the piece against the corner of the fence and slowly pivot it into the cut.

[10] CUTTING THE PROFILE

Once the cutting board is against the fence, slowly rotate it counterclockwise to make the cut. After you make a complete revolution, carefully pivot the piece out of the cut. Repeat the process to cut the profile on the other side, changing the cutter if you desire. Sand and finish the cutting board. As with the squircle cutting board, I usually use an oil-varnish blend as a finish. Once the finish thoroughly dries the solvents evaporate, leaving a food-safe coating.

RICHARD RHODES
FARM
table saw
table saw tips & tricks
band saw tips & tricks
SMART WORKSHOP SOLUTIONS

BOOKSHELVES [3]

It is the rare house that doesn't need a set of bookshelves. Whether to house your woodworking library or display your collection of vintage Star Wars memorabilia, everyone needs at least a few shelves to store and/or display his treasured possessions. All too often, however, bookcases are blocky, tippy affairs that lack much in the way of visual style.

This set of shelves answers both dilemmas. Rather than having sides, two tapered uprights that set in from the edges support the shelves. This serves to give the unit a lighter, airier look and makes for better display areas at the ends of the shelves. Having the shelves narrow toward the top helps with the tipping problem as it distributes the weight toward the rear. It also creates a natural hierarchy for display—larger, heavier things fit best on the bottom shelves while lighter, smaller items take the top. This makes sense from both an aesthetic and safety point of view.

The shelves are joined to the uprights with lap joints. These are fairly straightforward to cut, although you do have to accommodate the angled sides. My piece has ash uprights and cherry shelves. It is finished with several coats of wiping varnish.

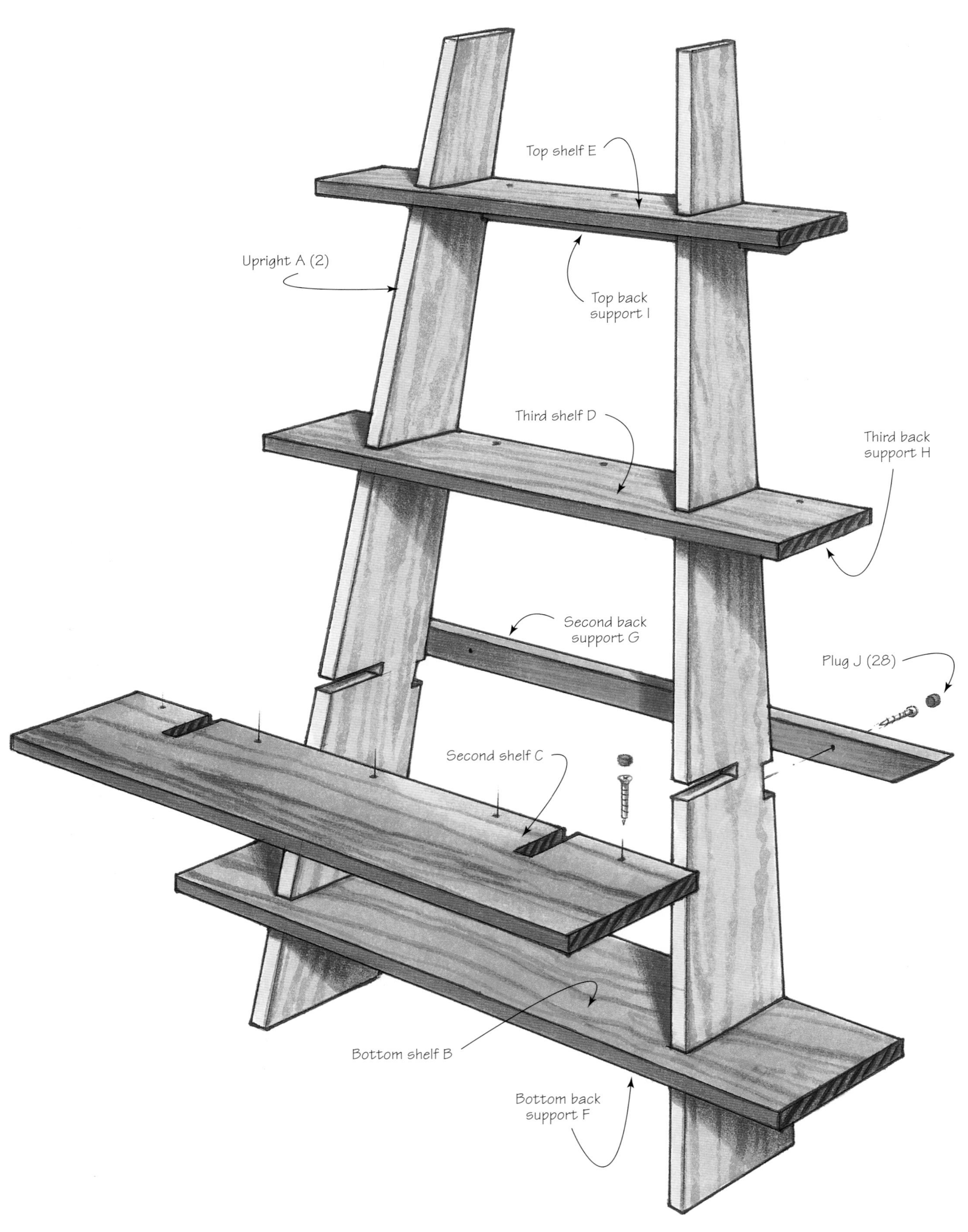
Top shelf E
Upright A (2)
Top back support I
Third shelf D
Third back support H
Second back support G
Plug J (28)
Second shelf C
Bottom shelf B
Bottom back support F

[BOOKSHELVES] inches (millimeters)

REFERENCE	QUANTITY	PART	STOCK	THICKNESS	(mm)	WIDTH	(mm)	LENGTH	(mm)	COMMENTS
A	2	uprights	hardwood	7/8	(22)	11	(280)	65	(1651)	
B	1	bottom shelf	hardwood	3/4	(19)	11 3/4	(298)	40 5/8	(1031)	
C	1	second shelf	hardwood	3/4	(19)	10	(254)	37 7/8	(962)	
D	1	third shelf	hardwood	3/4	(19)	8 1/4	(209)	35 1/8	(892)	
E	1	top shelf	hardwood	3/4	(19)	6 1/2	(165)	32 3/8	(822)	
F	1	bottom back support	hardwood	3/4	(19)	1 5/8	(41)	38 5/8	(981)	
G	1	second back support	hardwood	3/4	(19)	1 5/8	(41)	35 7/8	(911)	
H	1	third back support	hardwood	3/4	(19)	1 5/8	(41)	33 1/8	(841)	
I	1	top back support	hardwood	3/4	(19)	1 5/8	(41)	30 3/8	(771)	
J	28	plugs	hardwood							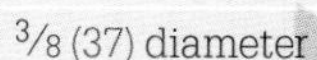 3/8 (37) diameter

[HARDWARE]

28 8 × 1 5/8" (20cm × 4cm) Screws

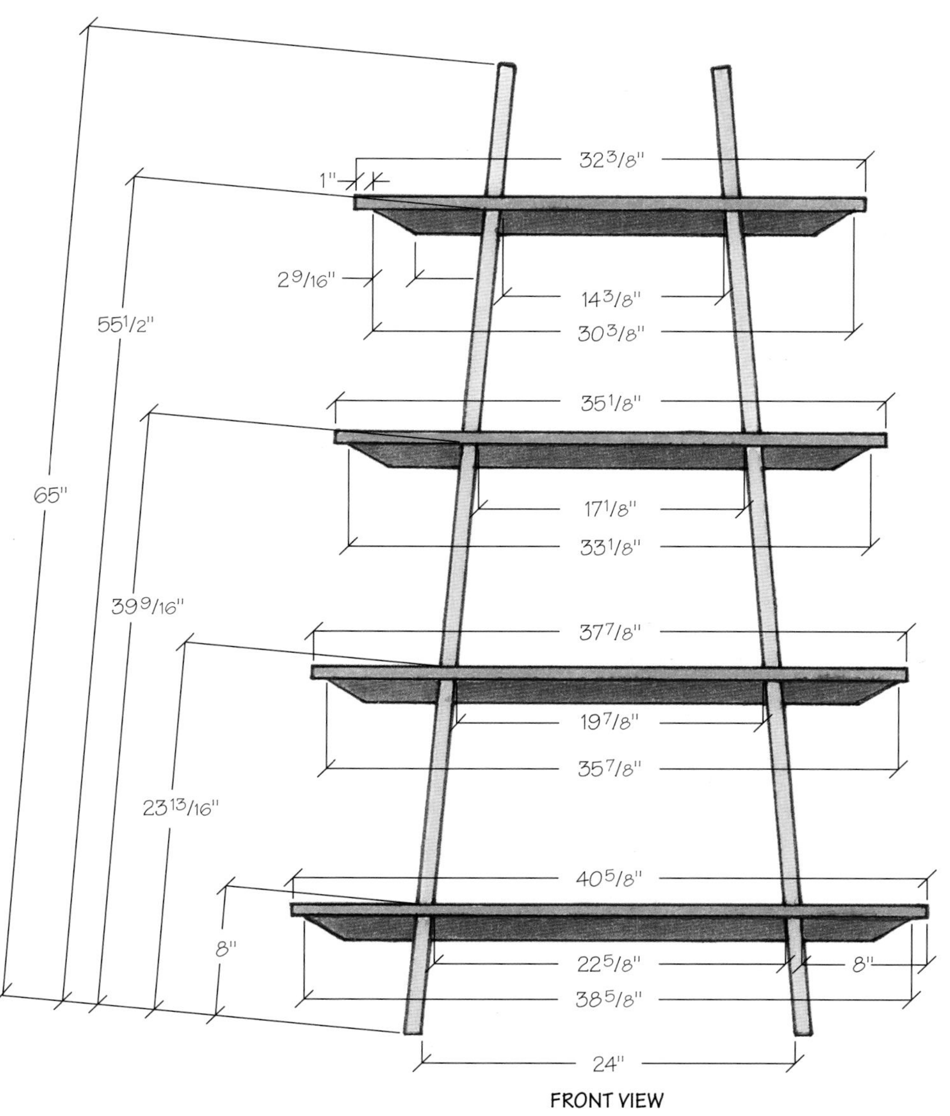

FRONT VIEW

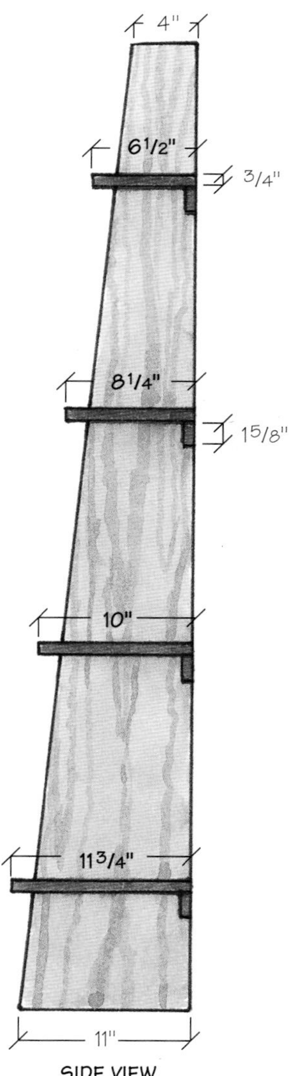

SIDE VIEW

[1] CUT THE UPRIGHTS
Cut the uprights to the size given in the materials list. Lay out the taper on one of the pieces. I didn't have a carrier board that was large enough to accommodate these pieces. Instead I attached a straightedge to the top of the workpiece parallel to the cut line and ran it along the fence to guide the cut. Align the straightedge on the upright with one edge ½" (12mm) to the waste side of the cut line. Screw the straightedge to the waste part of the upright, keeping the screws well away from the edge. Adjust the fence so the distance between it and the blade matches the width of the straightedge. Guide the straightedge along the fence to make the cut. Repeat the process with the second upright.

[2] CUT AND LAY OUT THE SHELVES
Cut the shelves to the sizes listed. Set up a dado blade that matches the thickness of the shelves. Tilt the blade on the saw to an 85° angle. Lay out the shelf locations on both sides of the uprights. Be sure to account for the angle as you make the layout. Also be sure to make a left and a right side. Depending on which way your saw tilts, you can cut one side or the other with the back edge of the piece against the miter gauge with the miter gauge set square to the blade. At each shelf location, mark the center of the upright then cut until you are ¼ inch (6mm) from the mark. Carefully back the piece out of the cut.

[3] MAKE THE CUTS FOR THE TOP SHELVES
Because of the way the rules of geometry work, you can actually turn the piece over to make the cuts for the top two shelves without having to change the angle of the blade. Make these cuts. Then cut the notches back to the center marks with a sharp chisel. This will leave about a ⅛" (3mm) flat on the pieces instead of a fragile knife edge. Note: I found it easier to keep the piece aligned with the layout lines if I clamped it to the miter gauge to keep it from shifting.

[4] MAKE THE ANGLED SHELF NOTCHES
To make the angled shelf notches on the second upright, the front (tapered) edge must be against the miter gauge. But because this edge is cut at an angle and the notches must be square to the back edge, you'll have to tilt the miter gauge to compensate. Adjust the gauge to make the back edge of the upright square to the blade.

[5] CUT THE SLOTS IN THE SECOND UPRIGHT
To cut the slots in the second upright, align the layout marks with the blade and clamp the upright to the miter gauge. Lower the blade beneath the table. Push the upright over the blade with the miter gauge. Try to position the upright so the center mark is about 1" (25mm) beyond the saw arbor. Start the saw, then slowly raise the blade. Stop cranking when the cut is about 1/4" (6mm) from the center mark.

[6] COMPLETE THE CUT AND TRIM
Push the upright forward to complete the cut. Trim the end of the cut back to the halfway mark with a sharp chisel as you did with the first upright. Note: The shelves are cut in similar manner—I discovered as I was notching them that it helped to clamp a stop block behind the miter gauge to help hold it in place as I raised the blade. You can see this in step eight. If I were to make this piece again, I would use the stop block for the notches in the uprights as well.

[7] CUT NOTCHES ON THE SHELVES

Lay out the notches on the top and bottom shelves. Also measure the depth of the notches on the uprights and transfer this measurement to the shelves. The first cut on each shelf is made conventionally with the dado set at the same angle you used for the uprights. Hold the shelf with its front edge against the miter gauge. Align the blade with the layout lines and push the shelf into the cut. Stop about 1/4" (6mm) from the depth mark. Unless you have an extremely wide dado blade, you'll have to make these notches in several passes. Note: Unlike the uprights, the shelves are small enough to control without clamping the pieces to the miter gauge but feel free to use a clamp for the added control it provides.

[8] MAKE THE SECOND CUTS

For each shelf's second cut, you'll need to raise up the blade through the piece as you did with the second upright. Note the stop block clamped to the table behind the miter gauge. This is particularly useful as you'll need to repeat each cut several times to make the notches wide enough. Once you have the top and bottom shelves notched, fit the unit together so you can double-check the measurements for the middle two shelves.

[9] SCREW THE FENCES TO THE CARRIER BOARD

Switch back to a regular saw blade set square to the table. Cut the back supports to the sizes listed. Lay out the angled cut on the end of one of the pieces. Place the piece on a carrier board that has a cut up the center, aligning the layout line with the edge of the cut. Screw fences to the carrier board to hold the piece in position. Cut both ends of each back support.

Need a Wider Straightedge?

To taper with the aid of a straightedge, the straightedge has to be wider than the waste piece, right? Not necessarily. It is true that if the waste piece is wider than the straightedge, some of it may stick out and interfere with the cut. However, instead of finding a wider straightedge, all you need do is cut off the part of the waste that sticks out.

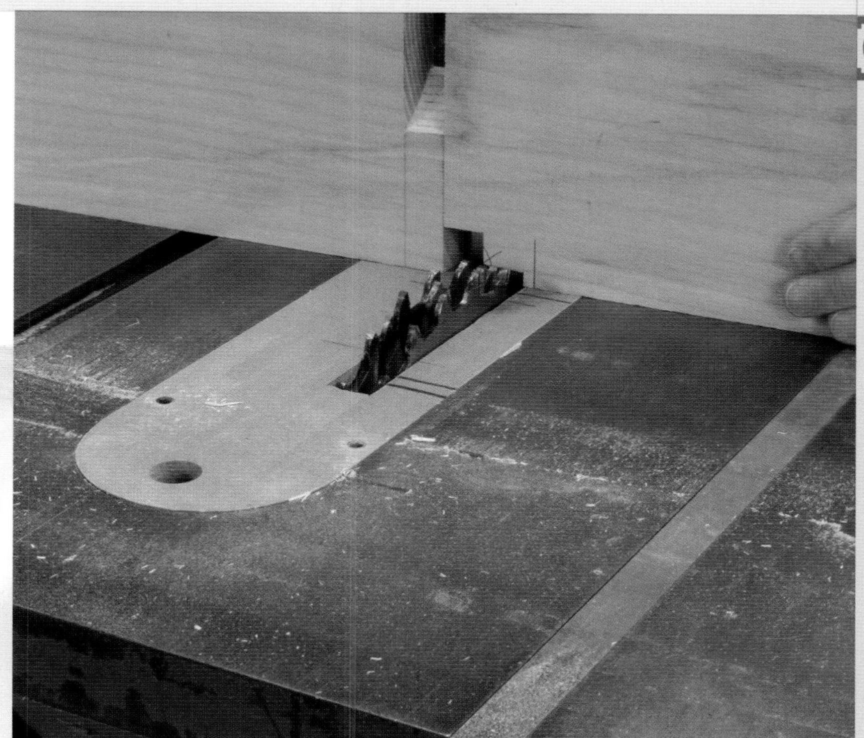

[10] ATTACH THE BACK SUPPORTS
The back supports fit into notches cut in the back edges of the uprights. Set up as wide a dado as possible and set its height equal to the thickness of the back supports. Lay out the notches just under where the shelves will be. Make the notches by guiding the pieces past the blade with the miter gauge. Note: On one of the uprights, the miter gauge should angle 5° toward the blade. On the other, the gauge should angle 5° away from the blade.

[11] ADD THE COUNTERBORE HOLES TO THE SHELVES
Drill and counterbore holes along the back edges of the shelves for the screws that will attach the shelves to the back supports.

[12] FINISH THE UNIT
Sand all the pieces, then fit the shelves into their notches in the uprights. Fit the back supports into their notches, predrilling the holes for the screws and counterboring for plugs. Screw the back supports to the uprights, then screw the shelves to the supports. Plug the holes and sand the plug flush. Add any final flourishes you wish

WINDY RIDGE WOODWORKS

GAME BOX

[4]

The first project in my beginning woodworking classes is often a box—but not a generic box. I require students to design a box that holds something specific, such as this one. I designed it as a wedding present for some of my colleagues. It has special compartments to hold two decks of cards, a set of six dice, a score pad and pen (advertising my shop, Windy Ridge Woodworks, of course), and two other card games my family and I particularly enjoy (Skipbo and Split). The dice are for a game I learned several years ago that I know simply as "Dice." I include the rules in the box with the rest of the game supplies and have reproduced them here on page 49 for you to enjoy as well. Of course, you should feel free to customize the box and include your favorite games in place of mine.

Building the box is pretty straightforward. The corners of both the main box and the tray are joined with finger joints. The box and the tray bottoms are trapped in grooves cut in the box and tray sides. The lid is a frame and panel assembly joined with slip joints at the corners. The lid's panel is a little unusual, as it overlaps the front of the frame. I made my box from luan (Philippine mahogany) that I had leftover from another project, but almost any hardwood is suitable.

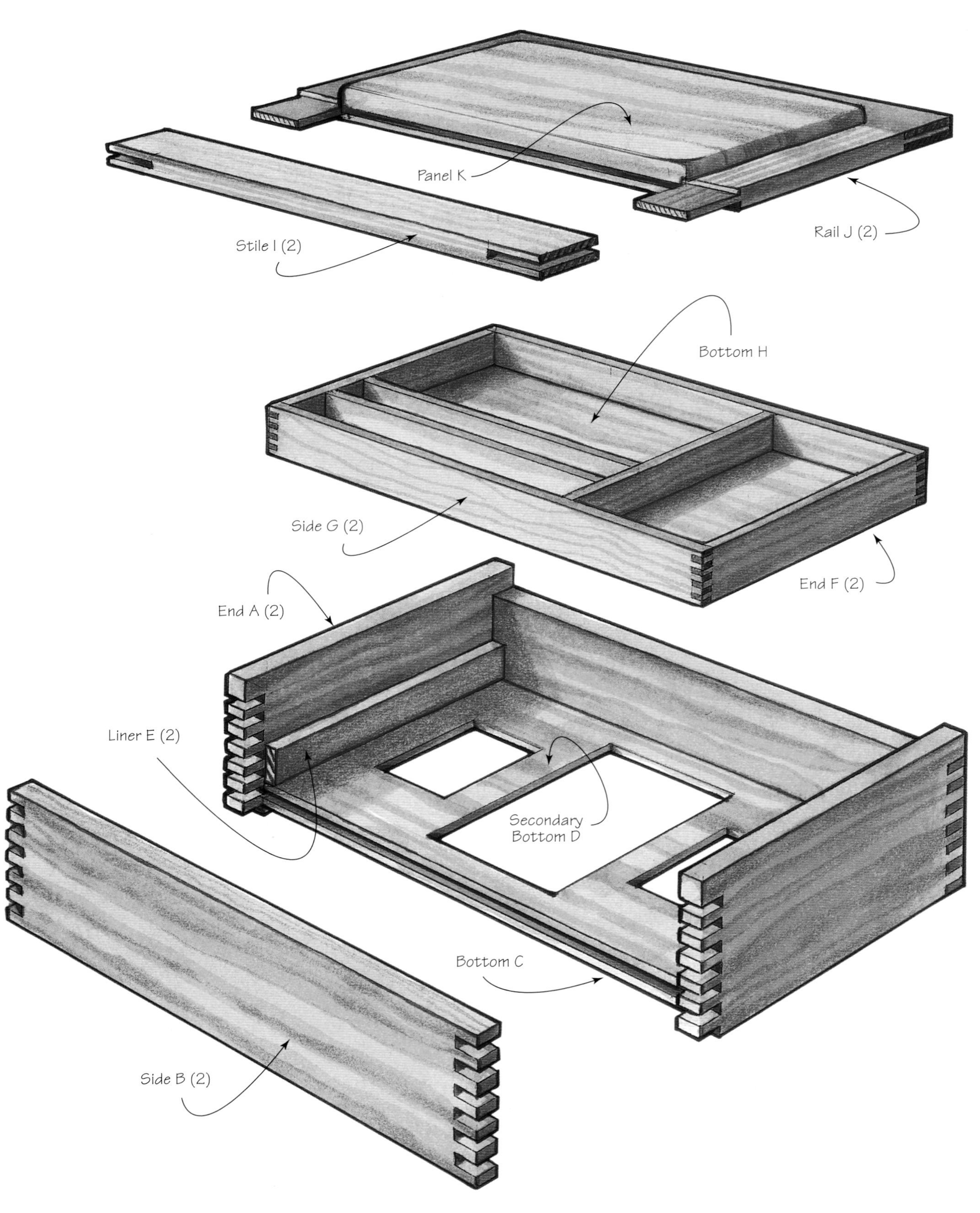
Panel K
Rail J (2)
Stile I (2)
Bottom H
Side G (2)
End F (2)
End A (2)
Liner E (2)
Secondary
Bottom D
Bottom C
Side B (2)

[BOX] inches (millimeters)

REFERENCE	QUANTITY	PART	STOCK	THICKNESS	(mm)	WIDTH	(mm)	LENGTH	(mm)	COMMENTS
A	2	ends	hardwood	7/16	(11)	3 3/4	(95)	7 5/8	(194)	
B	2	sides	hardwood	7/16	(11)	3 1/4	(82)	13 1/8	(333)	
C	1	bottom	hardwood	3/16	(5)	7	(178)	12 1/2	(317)	Can use 1/8" (3mm) plywood.
D	1	secondary bottom	hardwood	3/16	(5)	7	(178)	12 1/2	(317)	Can use 1/8" (3mm) plywood
E	2	liners	hardwood	1/4	(6)					

[TRAY]

REFERENCE	QUANTITY	PART	STOCK	THICKNESS	(mm)	WIDTH	(mm)	LENGTH	(mm)	COMMENTS
F	2	ends	hardwood	7/16	(11)	3 3/4	(95)	7 5/8	(194)	
G	2	sides	hardwood	7/16	(11)	3 1/4	(82)	13 1/8	(333)	
H	1	bottom	hardwood	3/16	(5)	7	(178)	12 1/2	(317)	Can use 1/8" (3mm) plywood

[LID]

REFERENCE	QUANTITY	PART	STOCK	THICKNESS	(mm)	WIDTH	(mm)	LENGTH	(mm)	COMMENTS
I	2	stiles	hardwood	1/2	(13)	1 3/8	(35)	7 5/8	(194)	
J	2	rails	hardwood	1/2	(13)	1 3/8	(35)	12 1/4	(311)	
K	1	panel	hardwood	1/2	(13)	5 5/8	(136)	10 1/4	(260)	

[HARDWARE]

1 — 3/4" × 1 1/2" (19mm × 38mm) Pair Hinges

12 — 4" × 3/8" (9mm) Brass Screws

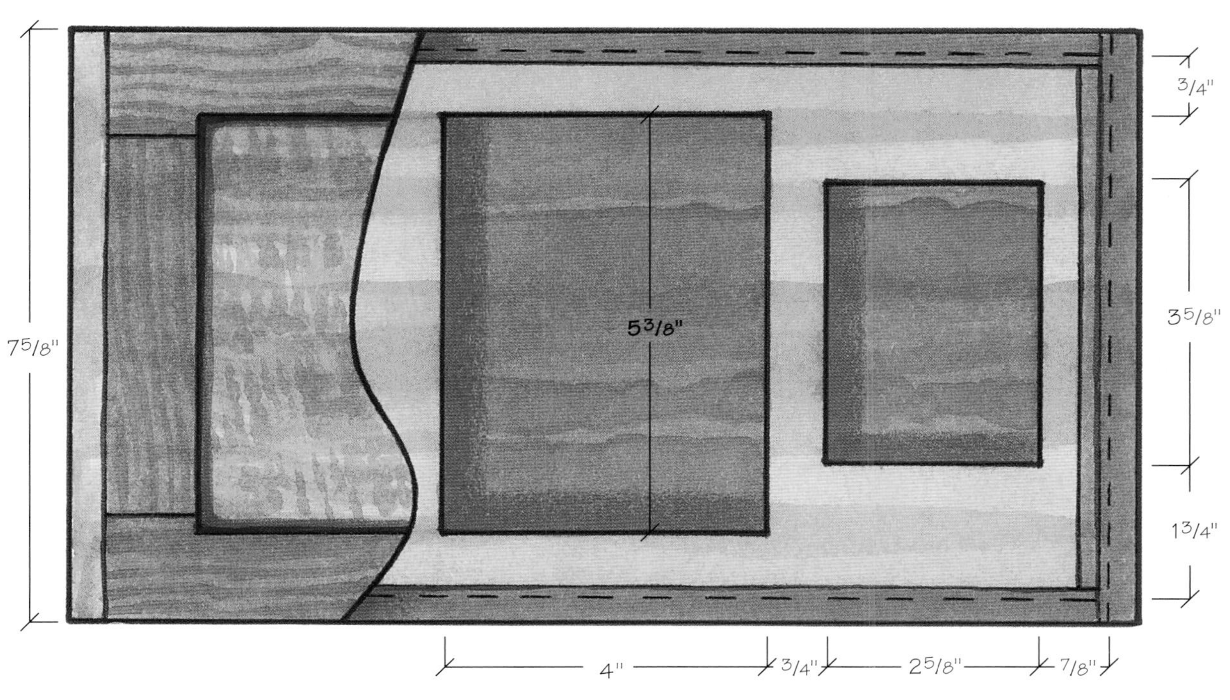

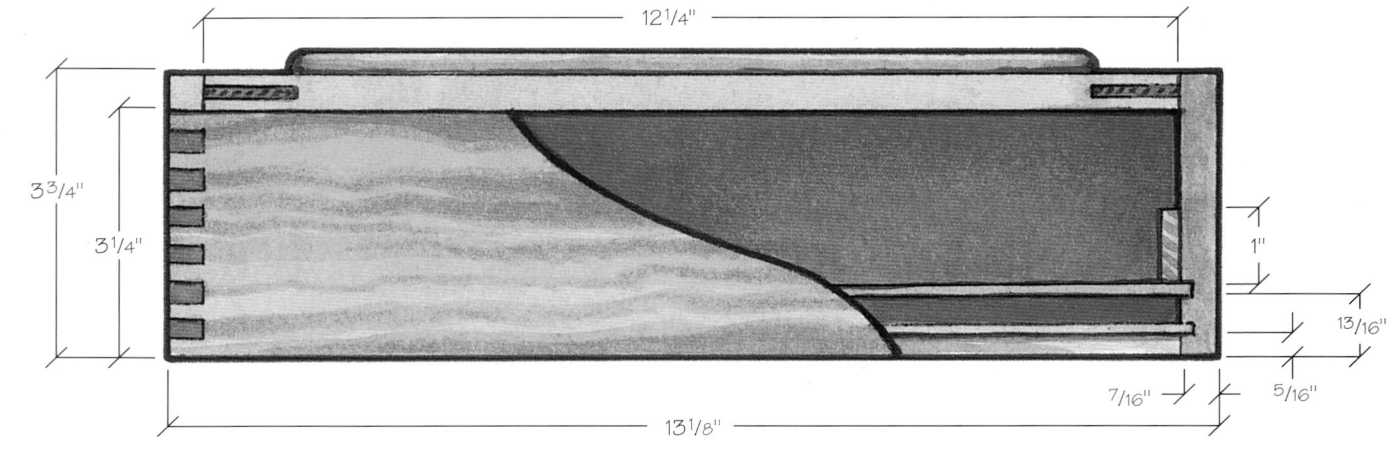
12 1/4"
3 3/4"
3 1/4"
1"
13/16"
7/16"
5/16"
13 1/8"

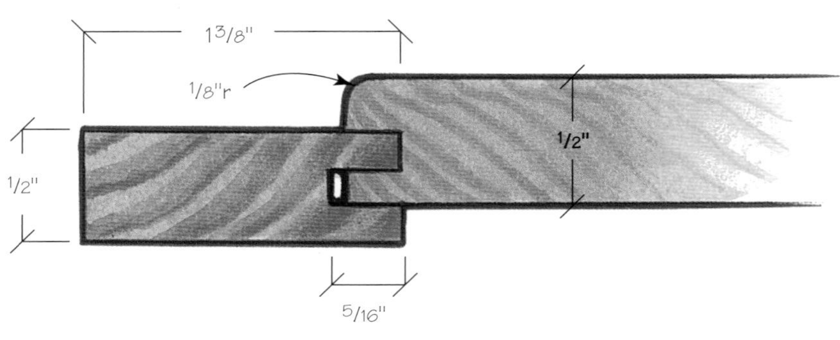
1 3/8"
1/8"r
1/2"
1/2"
5/16"

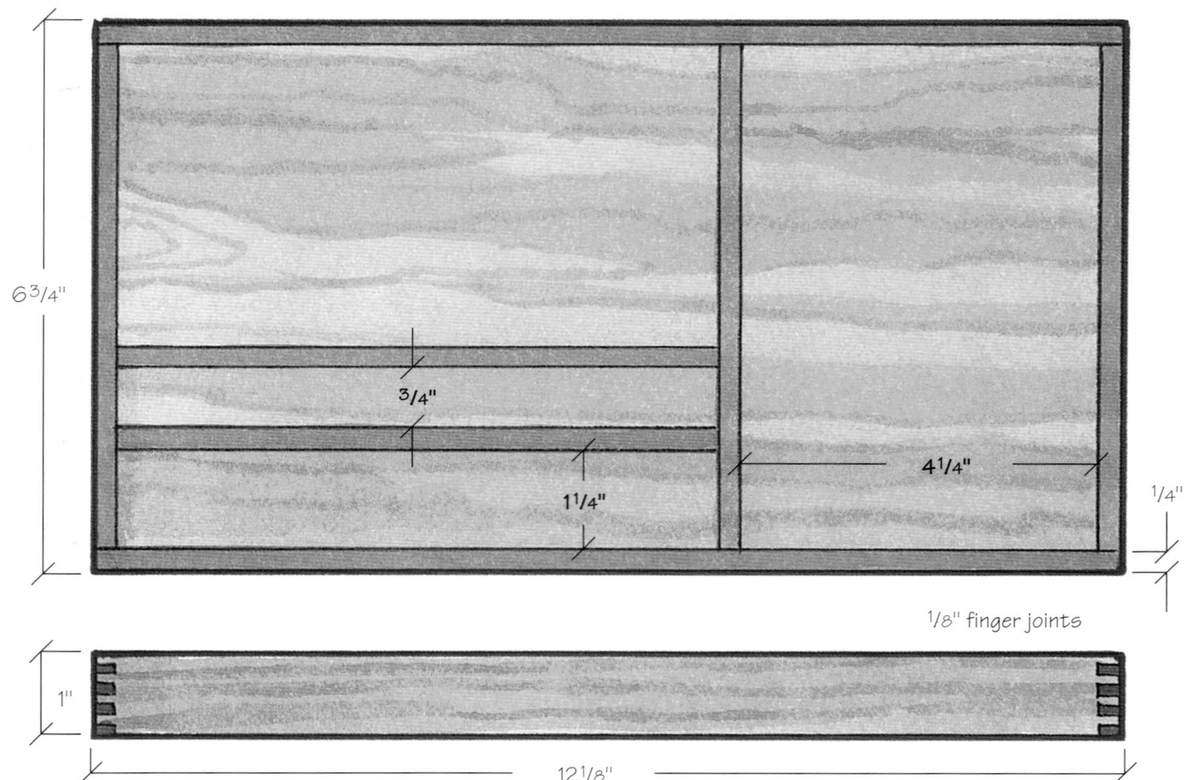
6 3/4"
3/4"
1 1/4"
4 1/4"
1/4"
1/8" finger joints
1"
12 1/8"

[1] CUT A PIECE TO LENGTH

Cut the pieces for the box and tray to the sizes specified in the materials list. Rip the pieces to width first, then cut them to length. I always cut one end of each piece square and stack the pieces with the square ends facing away from me on the saw table. Then I set up a stop and saw the other ends square, cutting the pieces to length in the process.

[2] CUT FINGER JOINTS ON AN END

Cut the corner joints for the box. Cut the ends first, starting with their bottom edges against the jig's key. Stop the cuts when you get to $^1/_2$" (13mm) of the top edge. Repeat the process with the side pieces, starting these pieces with a cut rather than a finger (see "cutting finger joints" on page 57).

[3] CUT THE GROOVES FOR THE BOTTOMS

Swap the finger joint setup for a rip blade and cut the grooves for the two bottoms in the end and side pieces. This process creates notches in the ends of the sides that will be visible in the finished piece. Rather than trying to make a stopped cut, I simply fill these notches with small pieces of wood after assembly.

[4] RABBET A BOTTOM PANEL

If you use hardwood for the bottom panels, you'll probably have to rabbet the edges so they fit in their grooves. Cut these rabbets by running the pieces vertically past the blade. Be sure to hold the pieces as flat as possible as they run along the fence so the resulting tongue has a consistent thickness.

[5] ROUT THE OPENINGS FOR THE CARDS

There are a few things the table saw doesn't do well. Making the cutouts for the games is one of them. Instead, make these cuts with a 1⁄4" (6mm) straight bit in a router table. Lay out the openings to suit the games you intend to include. Make the cuts by first tipping the piece onto the running bit, then running the piece along the fence from right to left. Reposition the fence as necessary to make the required cutouts.

[6] GLUE THE BOX

Sand the two bottoms and the inside surfaces of the sides and ends. Pre-finish the bottoms (at least one coat). Put the box together after spreading glue on all the mating surfaces of the fingers. Clamping is a lot easier if you make a set of box clamps.

[7] CUT FINGER JOINTS IN THE TRAY PIECES

It's important that you cut the pieces for the tray to fit snugly inside the box—by the time you fit the joints and sand everything, you'll create a little clearance. Cut finger joints to join the corners of the tray. If possible, use a rip blade to make the cuts as it leaves a square cornered kerf. Note: I made a separate jig to cut 1⁄8"-wide (3mm) fingers, but you could easily use the same jig you have for 1⁄4" (6mm) fingers. Just flip the fences upside down and make a new slot and key for the narrower blade. The advantage to having two separate jigs is that once you have them adjusted, they stay that way.

[8] CUT THE GROOVES FOR THE BOTTOM

Like the box bottom, the tray's bottom is captured in a groove that's cut in the tray's sides. Try hard to position the fence so the groove aligns with the fingers. If you're off by more than a hair, you'll have to patch both the sides and ends of the tray after glue-up.

[9] DOWEL THE DIVIDERS IN PLACE

Glue the tray together. When the glue dries, cut small square plugs to fill the bottom grooves and glue them in place. Cut pieces for the dividers. Size the dividers and the openings in the tray to suit your purposes. Position the dividers within the tray. Drill 1⁄8" (3mm) holes into the ends of the dividers and dowel them in place. You may find it helpful to cut spacers to go in between the dividers to maintain the proper spacing.

[10] MARK THE LID PIECES FOR REASSEMBLY

Cut the stiles and rails for the lid frame to size (cut a few extras just in case). Arrange the four best pieces the way you want the frame to go together. Mark the pieces with triangular marks as shown, with the open sides of the marks toward the inside of the frame.

Reference Surfaces

Occasions will arise when you'll want to make a cut that is centered on your workpiece. An example is the groove for the panel in the Game Box lid. The temptation is to make one cut, with one side of the piece against the fence, then turn the piece around and run it a second time with the opposite side against the fence. This will work, but if your workpieces vary at all in thickness, the resulting grooves won't be consistent.

My preference is to set the fence for the first cut. Cut all the pieces. Then reset the fence and make the second cut, running the same side of the workpiece against the fence. By using the same side of the workpiece as a reference surface for all cuts, your results will be consistent even if the dimensions of your workpieces are not.

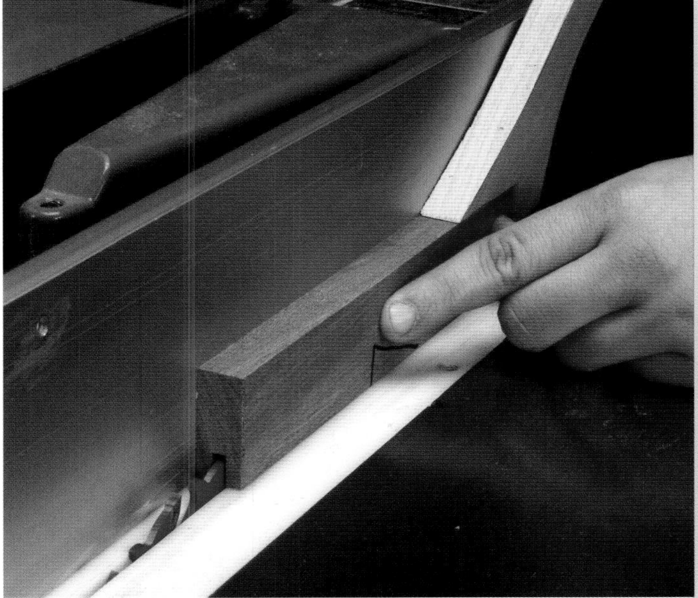

[11] CUT THE GROOVE FOR THE PANEL IN THE LID

Cut the groove for the lid's panel in two passes. Start with the fence 3⁄16" (5mm) away from the blade and the blade raised about 5⁄16" (8mm) above the table. Cut the pieces with their marked side away from the fence. After making the first cut in all of the pieces, bump the fence away from the blade, widening the cut to 3⁄16" (5mm). Be sure to cut grooves in your test pieces as well.

[12] SET THE HEIGHT OF THE BLADE FOR THE SLOT IN THE STILES

The corners of the lid frame are joined with a slip joint (also called a bridle joint or an open mortise and tenon). In this joint, tongues cut on the ends of the rails fit into slots cut in the ends of the stiles. Start by cutting the slots in the stiles. Use a rip blade, if possible, as it will leave a square-bottomed kerf. Set the blade height equal to the width of the rails less slightly more than the depth of the groove.

[13] CUT THE SLOT IN THE STILE

Clamp a stile in the simple tenoning jig with the marked side facing away from the jig and the groove facing the blade. Adjust the rip fence so the blade cuts along the fence side of the groove. Cut all the pieces with the marked side facing out. Then readjust the fence so the blade cuts along the opposite side of the groove, creating a slot $^{3}/_{16}$" (5mm) wide. Make the second cut in all the pieces. Note: I rarely make test-cuts for the stiles, as I'll be cutting the rails to fit whatever size slot I end up with.

[14] CUT THE TONGUES ON THE RAILS

To cut the tongues on the rails, raise the blade height to slightly less than the width of the stiles. Because the cuts required are slightly wider than the width of the blade, you'll need to make them with two passes. The first pass, on the outside of the pieces, simply removes the excess material. Clamp a test rail into the jig and adjust the fence so the blade cuts along the face of the jig—don't worry if you actually cut into the jig a little. Turn the piece around in the jig (no need to worry about precision yet) and cut the waste away from the second side. Repeat the process on the other ends of the rails.

[15] MAKE THE PRECISION CUTS

With the waste out of the way, you can concentrate on making the precision cuts. Clamp the test rails in the jig with the marked side out and the groove facing the blade. Adjust the fence so the blade just kisses the edge of the groove. Make the cut. Ideally you will leave a hair-thin bit of wood alongside the groove. Take the test piece out of the jig and compare it to one of the stiles. Make adjustments, if necessary, and make the first precision cut on all the pieces. Note: Be sure to load the pieces into the jig with the marked side out.

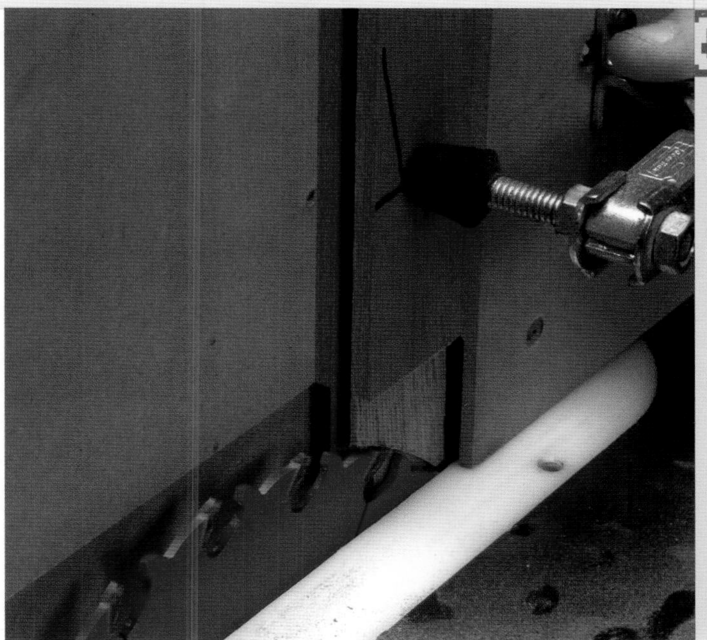

[16] MAKE THE SECOND PRECISE CUT

Reposition the fence to make the second precision cut. Again, your aim is to leave a hair-thin bit of wood alongside the groove. Cut the test piece and check the fit of the tongue in the slot. The pieces should go together with firm hand pressure. Adjust as needed, then cut all the pieces.

[17] ROUND THE PANEL

Assemble the lid frame without glue to check the fit of the joints and to measure for the panel. Cut the piece for the panel $3/4$" (19mm) larger than the frame opening in both width and length. Cut a $1/8$" (3mm) roundover on the edges of the panel. If you have the right cutters, you can do this with a molding head on the table saw. You can also use a roundover bit on a router table.

[18] CUT THE GROOVE IN THE PANEL

The panel has a groove cut around its edges that mates with the groove in the frame pieces. Cut this groove by running the panel past the blade on edge. Set the blade height to $7/16$" (11mm). Start with the fence $3/16$" (5mm) from the blade. Cut all four edges, then bump the fence over to widen the cut. Check the fit of the panel against the grooves in the frame pieces.

[19] CUT THE TONGUE ON THE PANEL DOWN

While the panel laps the top of the frame by 3⁄8" (9mm), the tongue that engages the grooves only projects about 1⁄4" (6mm) to allow the panel room for expansion. To cut the tongue down to size, reset the blade height to a hair more than 3⁄16" (5mm). Position the fence 1⁄32" (less than 1 mm) from the blade. Cut the tongue down on all four sides of the panel by running the panel along the fence.

[20] GLUE THE LID

Sand all the pieces, then glue the lid assembly together. When I glue up slip joints, I like to apply clamping pressure in all three directions.

[21] PIN THE PANEL IN PLACE

While the glue dries, make sure you can still move the panel within the frame. The whole idea behind frame and panel assembly is that the panel is free to move with changes in humidity. After you remove the clamps, center the panel. Drill two 1⁄8" (3mm) holes through the frame and into the edge of the panel. Place the holes in the center of each stile about 3⁄16" (5mm) in from the edge. Glue short pieces of 1⁄8" (3mm) dowel in the holes to keep the panel from shifting. By pinning the panel along its center line, you keep it from rattling around while still allowing it to expand to either side.

[22] HINGE THE LID

After pinning the panel in place, trim the lid to fit and hinge it to the back of the box. You can cut the mortises for the hinges by hand, or you can make up a C-shaped template to use with a handheld router equipped with a guide bushing and a 1⁄4" (6mm) straight bit. As an option, you might want to carve a finger recess along the front of the box to make it easier to open. Finish the box with your favorite wood finish. I gave the box in the photo several coats of Watco oil.

Dice

Dice is played with six dice. During each turn a player rolls all six dice and scores depending upon the combination of dots that appear. The first player to accumulate exactly 10,000 points wins.

Scoring is as follows:

Ones count as 100
Fives count as 50

The rest of the numbers don't count unless rolled in these combinations:

3 twos count as 200
3 threes count as 300
3 fours count as 400
3 sixes count as 600

In addition,

3 fives count as 500
3 ones count as 1000
3 pairs count as 1000
A straight (1, 2, 3, 4, 5, 6) also counts as 1000

During a turn, you roll all six dice. Set aside any that score. At this point you can either stop and collect your points or roll any nonscoring dice to try for more points. To qualify for a a combination, all the scoring dice must have been thrown in a single roll. For example, if on your first roll, you get 3 fives, they would score 500. However, if you get 2 fives on your first roll and 1 five on your second roll, your total would be only 150.

If you choose to roll more than once, you can roll only nonscoring dice the second time. The exception to this is if all of the dice score on the first roll. Then you can roll them all again (if you dare) for more points. If you roll the dice and none of them score, you forfeit any points earned that turn and your turn ends.

To begin the game and get on the scoreboard, you need to earn a minimum of 500 points in one turn. Keep score by simply maintaining a running total for each player. To win, you need to score exactly 10,000 points. If you go over, your score goes back to whatever it was at the end of your previous turn.

THE MACMILLAN
VISUAL DICTIONARY

BOOKSTAND

[5]

Whether you have an old family Bible to display or one of those big, fat dictionaries filled with words known only to English majors, you need to build one of these bookstands. Actually, the piece is more than a simple bookstand. The slanted surface is hinged, allowing excellent access to the compartment beneath, and the drawer makes a fine repository for pens, pencils and notepads.

Placed on a table in your library or study, the stand makes an excellent research station. Couple it with a base (the base shown here is detailed on page 70) and you'll have a fine stand-up desk. You could also use the stand in your entry as a place to sort incoming mail or in a spare bedroom as a home for your guest book. The bookstand also makes a nice place to display large format art books or other oversize publications that don't fit on regular bookshelves.

Construction is not complicated. The case is assembled with tongue-and-groove joints reinforced with screws. The drawer is put together with finger joints. The drawer face is glued on afterwards, giving the front finger joints the appearance of being half-blind. The stand in the photo is made of cherry with wenge plugs. The drawer sides and back are maple, and the drawer bottom is birch plywood. The outside is finished with several coats of wiping varnish, while the inside of the top compartment and the drawer are finished with shellac. Because the interior parts are shellaced, they smell much better than they would if you used varnish throughout.

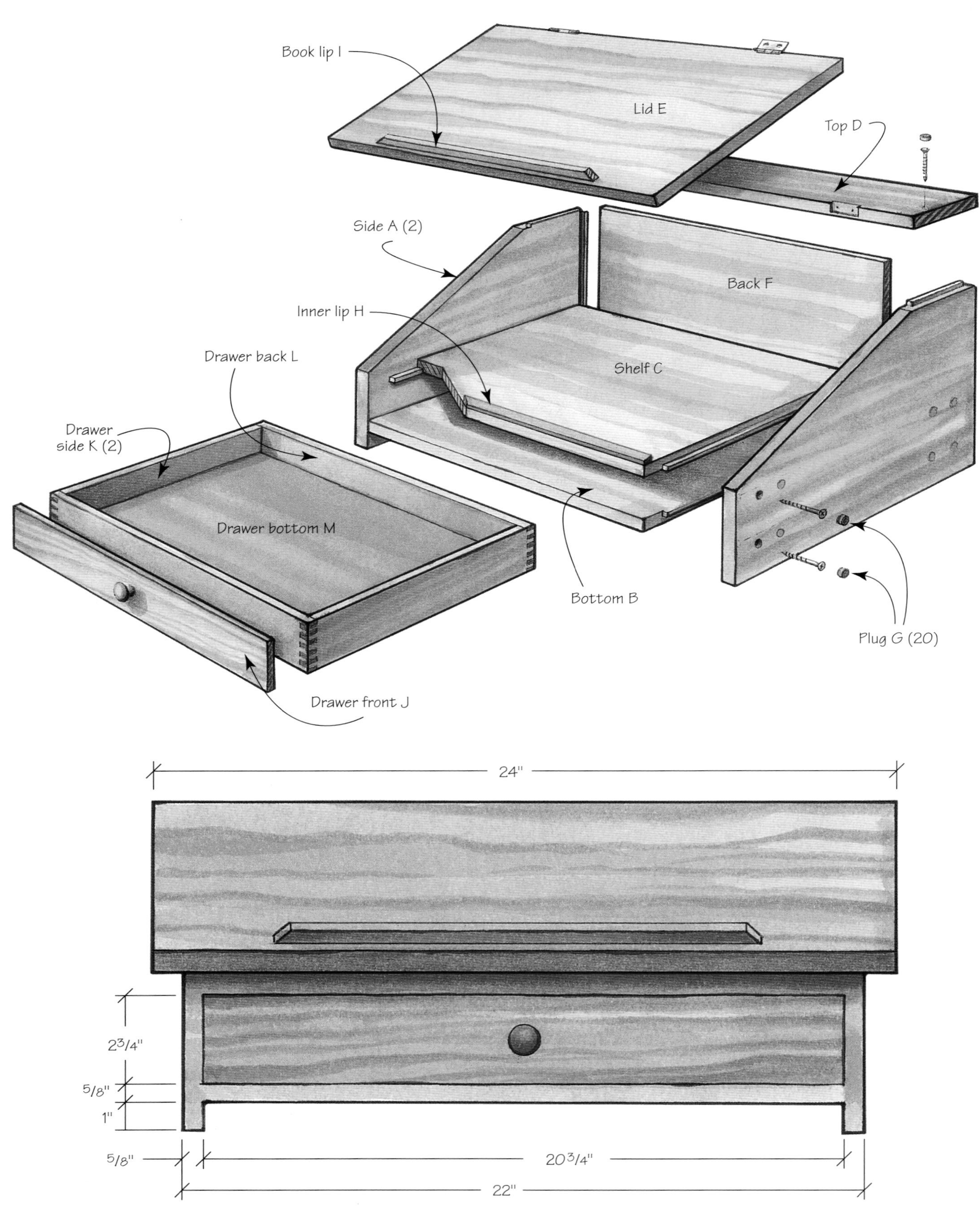

Book lip I
Lid E
Top D
Side A (2)
Back F
Inner lip H
Drawer back L
Shelf C
Drawer
side K (2)
Drawer bottom M
Bottom B
Plug G (20)
Drawer front J
24"
2 3/4"
5/8"
1"
5/8"
20 3/4"
22"

[BOOKSTAND] inches (millimeters)

REFERENCE	QUANTITY	PART	STOCK	THICKNESS	(mm)	WIDTH	(mm)	LENGTH	(mm)	COMMENTS
A	2	sides	hardwood	5/8	(16)	20	(508)	10 3/4	(273)	Make panels 1/2" (13mm) wider than necessary to start
B	1	bottom	hardwood	5/8	(16)	20	(508)	21 1/4	(540)	
C	1	shelf	hardwood	5/8	(16)	19 1/8	(486)	21 1/4	(540)	
D	1	top	hardwood	7/8	(22)	5	(187)	24	(610)	
E	1	lid	hardwood	7/8	(22)	16 3/4	(425)	24	(610)	
F	1	back	hardwood	5/8	(16)	9 1/4	(235)	21 1/4	(540)	
G	40	plugs	contrasting hardwood							3/8" (9mm) diameter
H	1	inner lip	hardwood	5/8	(16)	7/16	(11)	20 3/4	(527)	
I	1	book lip	hardwood	1/2	(13)	1/2	(13)	15	(381)	
J	1	drawer (front)	hardwood	7/8	(22)	2 3/4	(70)	20 3/4	(527)	Resaw before joinery
K	2	drawer (sides)	hardwood	1/2	(13)	2 3/4	(70)	18 1/2	(470)	
L	1	drawer (back)	hardwood	1/2	(13)	2 3/4	(70)	20 3/4	(527)	
M	1	drawer (bottom)	plywood	1/4	(6)	18	(457)	20 1/4	(514)	

[HARDWARE]

20	8 × 2 1/2" (203mm × 63mm) Screws
2	2 1/2 × 2" (63mm × 51mm) Extruded Brass Hinges w/Screws
1	1" (25mm) diameter Brass Knob

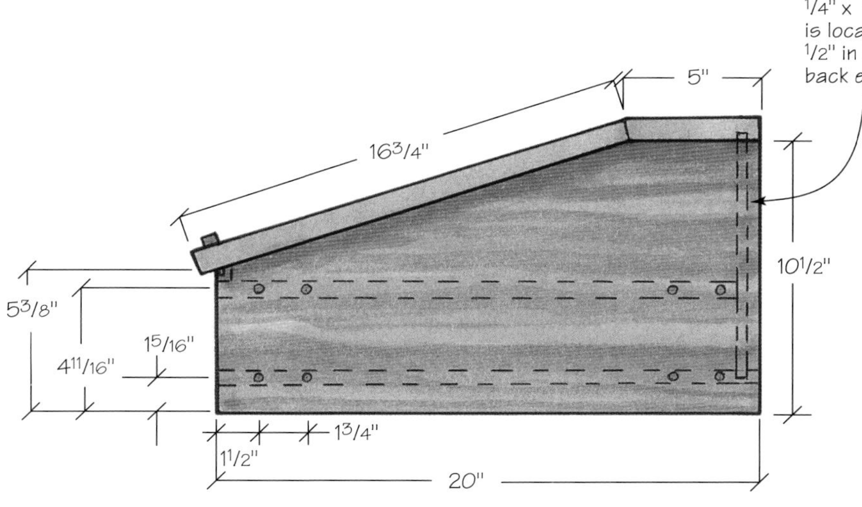

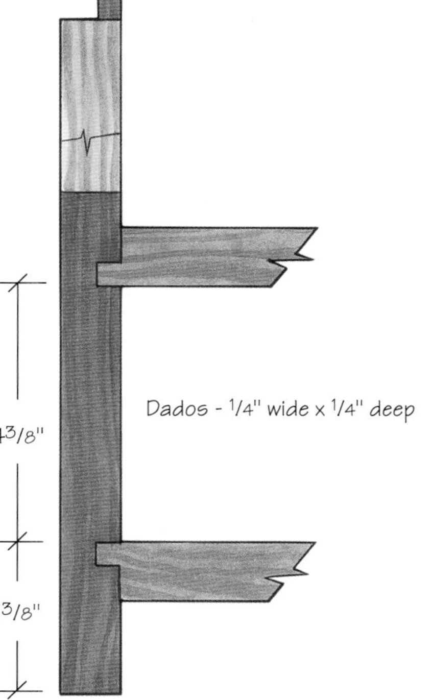

[1] CUT STRIP OFF PANEL
Edge-glue boards to make panels wide enough for the sides, bottom, and shelf. For the sides, I found it easier to glue up one long panel rather than two shorter ones. After the glue dries, rip a 1/2-wide (13mm) strip off both edges of the side panel. (You'll glue these back in place after cutting the dadoes for the bottom and shelf.) Crosscut the sides to length.

[2] CUT GROOVES ACROSS THE SIDES
Set up a 1/4"-wide (6mm) dado and set its depth of cut to 1/4" (6mm). Cut dadoes across the sides as shown in the Dado Detail. Glue the 1/2" (13mm) strips from step one back in place.

[3] CUT GROOVES ON THE BOTTOM
Increase the width of the dado to about 1/2" (13mm) and decrease its height a hair [about 1/32" (less than 1mm)]. Adjust the rip fence so it is slightly more than 1/4" (6mm) from the blade. Cut a tongue on the end of a piece of scrap and check its fit in one of the dadoes on one of the sides. Adjust the fence and recut until the tongue goes into the dado with firm hand pressure. Cut tongues on both ends of the shelf and bottom. Also cut a tongue on the top end of each side.

[4] CUT THE ANGLE ON THE SIDES
Lay out the angled cut on one of the sides. Place the side on a carrier board with layout line aligned with the carrier's edge. Screw fences to the carrier to hold the side in position. With a regular saw blade mounted on the saw, adjust the rip fence so the blade cuts right along its outer edge. Hold the side against the fences and make the cut. Repeat the process with the second side, but be sure to make it a mirror image of the first.

[5] CUT DADOS ACROSS THE TOP

Cut away the tongues on the shelf and the bottom 1/2" (13mm) in from the front edge (and from the back edge on the bottom piece). Clamp the sides to the shelf and bottom so you can get a real measurement for where the dadoes should go on the top. Cut the top to size, then cut ½" (13mm) strips off both edges of the top. Set up a 1/4" (6mm) dado and cut 1/4"-deep (6mm) dadoes across the top so that they correspond with the tongues on the sides. Glue the 1/2" (13mm) strips back in place.

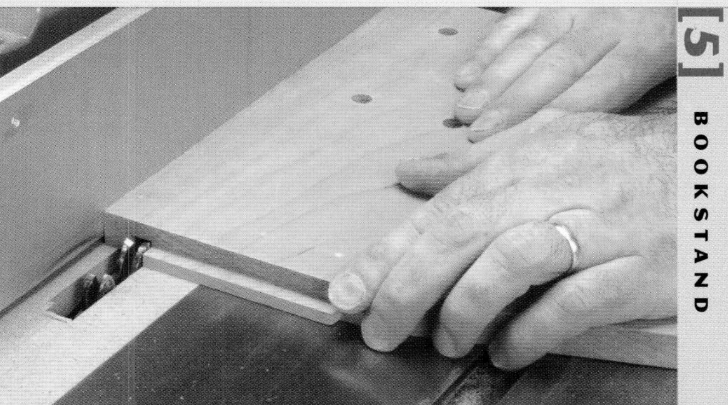

[6] DADO FOR THE BACK

Increase the width of the dado to 3/8" (9mm), but leave its height the same. Cut grooves for the back in the sides, bottom and top. The grooves will show at the bottom on the sides and at the ends of the top. Cut pieces to fill these gaps and glue them in place. Cut the back to size and rabbet its edges to fit in the grooves.

[7] BEVEL THE LID

Edge-glue boards to make up the panel for the lid. When the glue dries, cut the lid to size. Tilt the blade on your saw to an 81° angle and bevel one edge of the lid and the front edge of the top.

[8] SCREW THE PIECE TOGETHER

Drill 3/8" (9mm) holes for the plugs, and 3/16" (5mm) holes for the screws through the sides and top. Apply glue to the tongues and assemble the case. Drill pilot holes for the screws. I find the screws go in easier and are less likely to break if I put a little paraffin wax on them before I drive them home. Plug the holes with a contrasting hardwood.

Cutting Plugs Flush

I assemble a lot of the pieces I make with screws. They serve as clamps, helping to hold the joints together as the glue dries, and they add reinforcement. Most of the time, I cover the screw heads with contrasting wood plugs. Cutting these plugs flush with the surface can be a bit tricky. I find that if I try to cut them off with a chisel, they often break. Or if I try to saw them off, I end up scarring the surface surrounding the plug even if I use a flush cutting saw (one with no set to the teeth). The method that works best is to drill a hole in the center of a 4" × 6" (10cm × 15cm) card that matches the diameter of the plug. Then I drop the card over the plug and cut the plug off with my flush trim saw. The card serves as a shield to protect the surface around the plug. Then all it takes is a little sanding to make everything flush.

[9] CLAMP THE LIP IN PLACE

Cut the inner lip to size and bevel its top edge to match the slope of the sides. Rather than try to make it flush with the sides, I cut it a little shy of the mark, leaving a slight step between the pieces. Glue the lip along the front edge of the shelf.

[10] MARK THE LID WITH DOWEL CENTERS

Cut the book lip to size and bevel its ends at about a 70° angle. Drill a 1⁄4" (6mm) hole near either end for alignment dowels. Center the lip near the front edge of the lid and use dowel centers to transfer the location of the dowel holes. Drill the matching holes in the lid. Cut short sections of dowel to serve as alignment pins and glue the lip in place.

[11] MORTISE FOR THE HINGES

Mortise the lid and the top for the hinges that will connect the two. This is one of the few tasks that a table saw doesn't do well. While you can cut the mortises by hand, I find it easier to make a quick router template. The accompanying DVD demonstrates how to do this in detail (making the template is, in fact, a table saw operation). The only difference is that here, you'll bevel the fence to match the angle on the top and lid.

[12] RESAW THE DRAWER FRONT

Cut the drawer front slightly larger than the dimensions listed in the materials list. Resaw the drawer front, leaving the inside portion of the piece 1⁄2" (13mm) thick to receive the finger joints. Cut this inside piece to size, leaving the outer drawer face larger for now.

[13] CUTTING FINGER JOINTS

Cut the rest of the drawer parts to size, then set up to cut the finger joints at the corners. Cut the fingers on the front and back first. Start cutting each piece with its top edge against the jig's key. Cutting finger joints is demonstrated in full on the accompanying DVD.

[14] FINGER JOINTING

Cut the matching parts of the joint on the drawer sides. These pieces start with a space rather than a finger. To make it easier to position this first cut, reverse the drawer front so its top edge is toward the blade. Place it on the jig with the first notch straddling the key. Hold the drawer side with its top edge butted up against the drawer front. Make the first cut, then set the drawer front aside and continue cutting the notches across the drawer side. Repeat the process for both ends of each side.

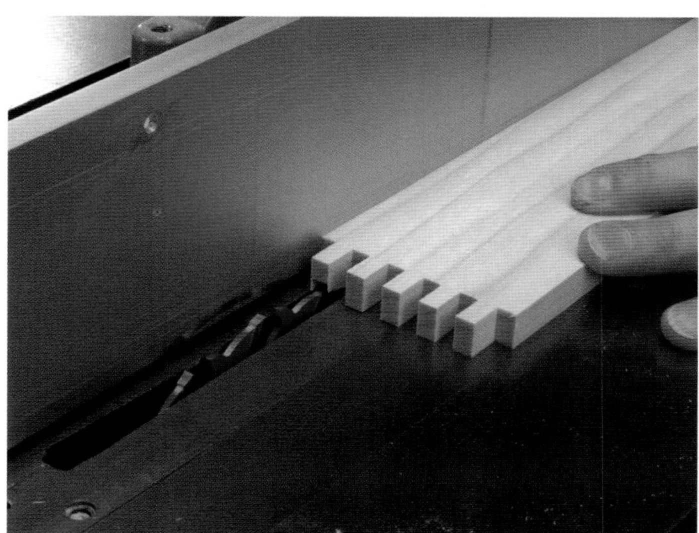

[15] CUTTING THE GROOVE FOR THE BOTTOM

Cut the groove for the bottom of all four drawer parts. Rather than using a dado blade, which is likely to be too wide for the plywood, make the groove with two passes of a regular saw blade. Position the groove so it coincides with one of the fingers on the drawer sides. This means the drawer face (when glued on) will cover the gap created. There will also be gaps at the back of the drawer, but these will be visible only if you pull the drawer all the way out.

[16] GLUING THE DRAWER FACE TO THE DRAWER

Glue the drawer together. Sand the drawer front flush and flat. To do so, I usually tape several fresh sheets of sand paper to the table saw table and scrub the drawer box across them. Glue the drawer face to the drawer front. Often I find my workbench makes a good flat place for such glue- ups. When the glue dries, sand the drawer and fit it to the opening. Glue a stop (a simple scrap of wood cut to whatever size you need) in the back of the drawer cavity so that the drawer ends up flush with the front of its opening. Finsh the bookstand with your favorite wood finish. The model in the photo is finished with several coats of wiping varnish.

MIRROR [6]

Mirrors are fun (and often profitable) to make because they go together relatively quickly, they don't require a lot of material and their function is built right in. Because most people like to look at themselves, their interest in mirrors is almost automatic.

The mirror featured here is very definitely of the twenty-first century, but its roots can be traced backwards more than two hundred years. Its scalloped pediment is closely related to that found on many Queen Anne and Chippendale pieces, and its "carved" vertical moldings recall the Victorian era. These elements combine with the vertical symmetry to create a look that is at home in many formal settings. The painted highlights, however, keep the piece from becoming stodgy.

The mirror frame is made from mahogany and has curly maple accents. The corners of the frame are put together with lap joints, and the mirror fits into rabbets cut in the backs of the frame pieces. You'll have to drill the circular cutout in the pediment or cut it with a band saw.

One of the most compelling parts of this project is the harlequin pattern cut into the side pieces. This is accomplished on the table saw using a molding head equipped with a V-cutter. A simple carriage guides the pieces through the cut at the appropriate angle. A small key governs the spacing of the grooves much the same way the spacing of the cuts is controlled when making finger joints. Once all the grooves are cut, add paint, then sand the surface to clean up any errant color. The colored dots are inlays of epoxy mixed with acrylic paint. Vary the color scheme to suit your décor.

Pediment C (2)
Mirror backer F
Frame panel
B (2)
Frame side
A (2)
Frame bottom
D (2)

[FRAME] inches (millimeters)

REFERENCE	QUANTITY	PART	STOCK	THICKNESS	(mm)	WIDTH	(mm)	LENGTH	(mm)	COMMENTS
A	2	frame sides	hardwood	1	(25)	2 1/4	(57)	39 1/4	(997)	
B	2	frame panels	contrasting hardwood	5/16	(8)	1 7/8	(48)	39 1/4	(997)	
C	2	pediment	hardwood	1 3/4	(44)	3 3/4	(95)	13 5/8	(346)	
D	2	frame bottom	hardwood	1 1/2	(38)	1 5/8	(41)	10 1/8	(257)	
E	2	spline	hardwood	5/16	(8)	1 3/4	(44)	1 1/2	(38)	
F	1	mirror backer	hardboard	1 1/8	(28)	18 3/4	(476)	42 1/4	(1073)	

[HARDWARE]

Mirror
Screw Eyes
Wire
Screws

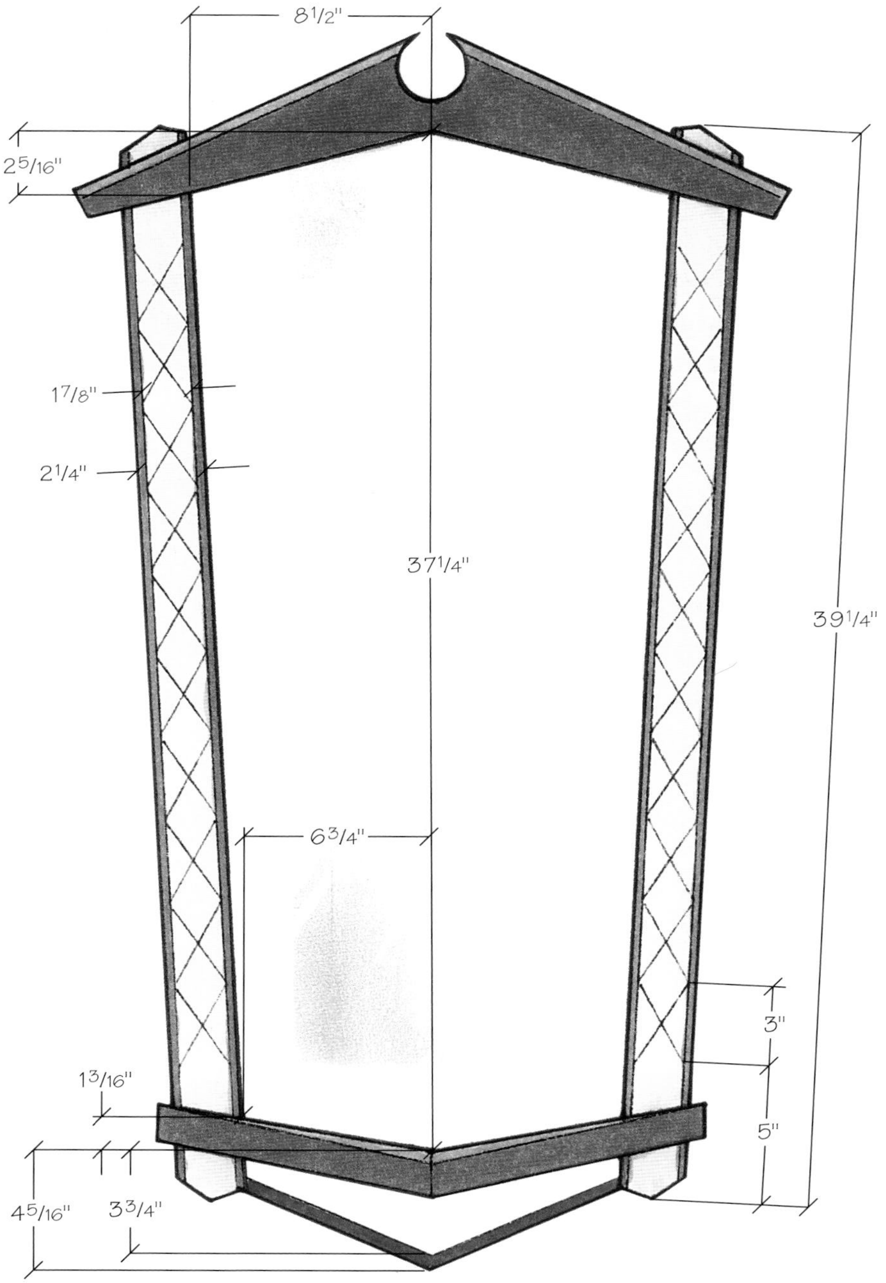

8 1/2"
2 5/16"
1 7/8"
2 1/4"
37 1/4"
39 1/4"
6 3/4"
3"
1 3/16"
5"
4 5/16"
3 3/4"

[1] DRAW THE FULL MIRROR

As with most projects that involve angles that are not 90° and pieces that taper, you'll find it much easier to measure and make your setups if you make a full-size drawing of the piece first. Start by drawing a center line, then use it as a reference for making the rest of the drawing.

[2] DADO THE FRAME SIDES

Cut the frame sides to the sizes given in the materials list. Set up a dado and cut a 1⁄8"-deep × 17⁄8"-wide (3mm × 48mm) channel down the center of each piece. This should leave 3⁄16" (5mm) of material on either side of the channels.

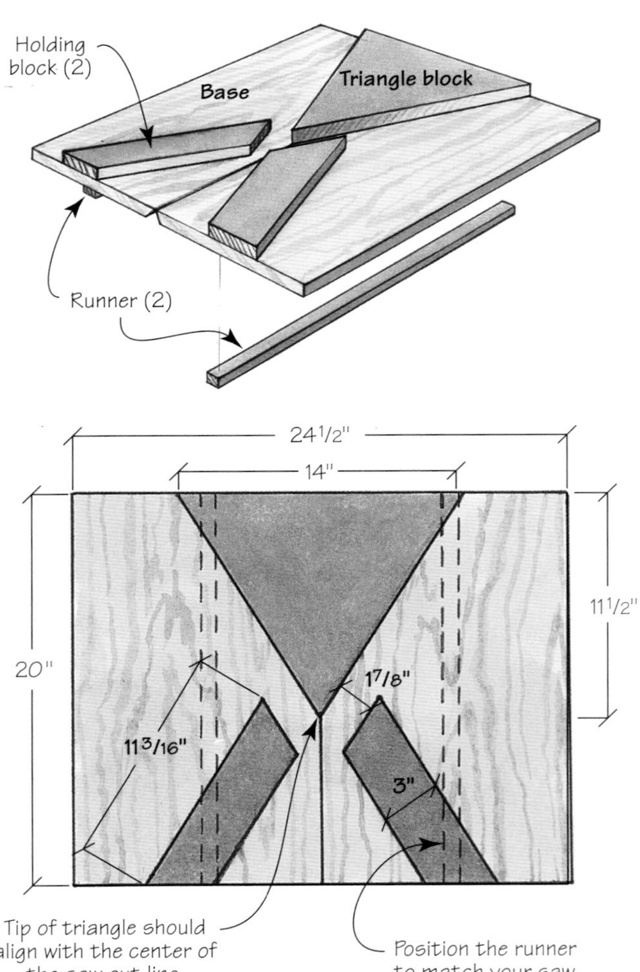

Drawing Materials

When I need to make a full-size drawing, I take a sheet of 1⁄8" (3mm) hardboard (or a portion thereof) and paint it white (or whatever leftover light color I happen to have). Then I make the drawing on the painted surface. If the piece is one I am likely to make again, I tuck the layout into my plywood rack for future reference. If the piece is one I am not likely to revisit, I paint over the drawing and save the sheet for a future drawing.

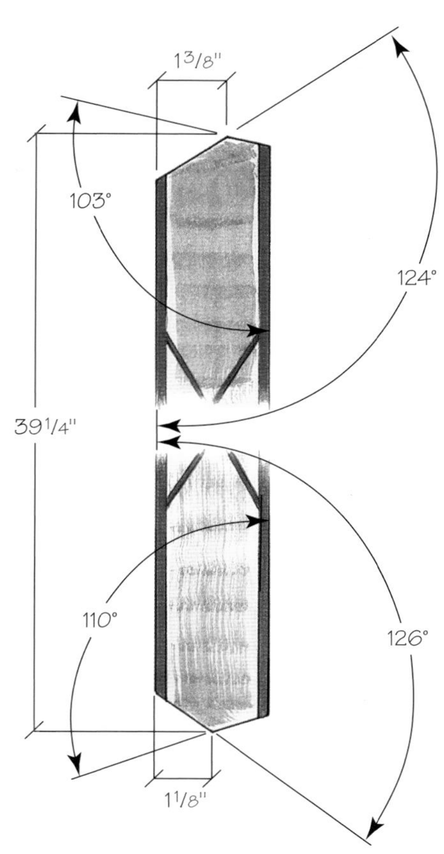

[3] RESAW THE PANELS

Cut the side panels to the size listed. Be careful to get the width right—the panels should fit snugly into the channels you cut in the frame sides. The pieces are thin enough to be resawn from a single piece of 4/4 material. Resaw the pieces, then open them up like a book to get grain patterns that are a near-perfect match.

[4] CUT THE HARLEQUIN PATTERN

Make up a sled, then set up a molding head with a V-cutter. Use the molding head to cut the slot in the sled—make the cut in several passes, raising the cutter a little with each pass. Stop when the tip of the V is about 1/16" (2mm) above the sled's surface. Start cutting the panels from the lower end first. Measure and position the first cut 5" (13cm) from the end.

[5] ADD THE BRAD

After you make the first cut in each panel, drive a small brad 3" (8cm) away from the cutter into the sled's surface. Leave the head slightly above the surface. This will serve to register each of the subsequent cuts. Make a total of 10 cuts across each of the panels. Be careful not to mar the pieces by dragging them over the brad.

[6] MARK THE PIECES FOR THE SECOND SET OF CUTS

Turn the pieces around for the second set of cuts. Remove the brad from the sled. Draw a perpendicular line across the panels from the end of the last cut to indicate where the second set of lines should begin. Make the first cut in each piece, then replace the brad and continue cutting.

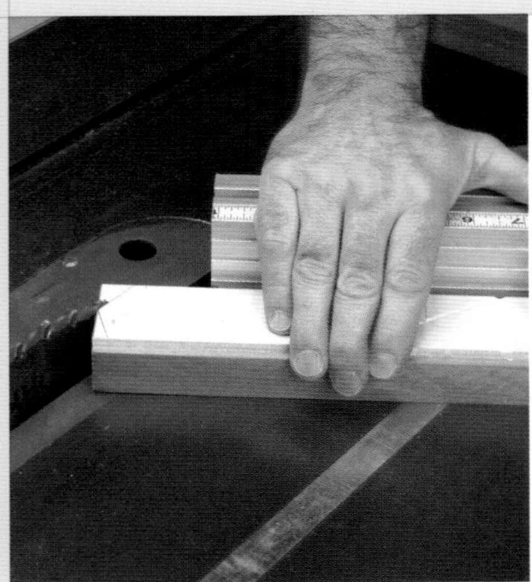

[7] CUT THE END OF ONE OF THE SIDE PIECES

Glue the panels in the channels cut in the frame sides. When the glue dries, cut the ends. Note: Be sure to make a right and a left side by cutting one frame side with the panel facing up and the second with the panel facing down. Position a stop along the miter gauge's fence to help maintain consistency.

[8] MITER THE PEDIMENT

Cut the pieces for the pediment to size. Crosscut one end of each at a 75° angle. Hold the pieces together and mark their outer faces.

[9] SLOT THE PEDIMENT PIECES

Set up a 5⁄16"-wide (8mm) dado and adjust it to make a 3⁄4"-deep (19mm) cut. Clamp a pediment piece in the simple tenoning jig with its marked side out. Position the rip fence so the dado will be centered across the thickness of the piece. Make the cut. Clamp the second piece in the jig with its marked side out, and cut it as well.

[10] MARK THE RABBETING SETUP, THE TABLE AND THE PEDIMENT

The mirror and the backing are contained in a stepped rabbet that's cut in the pediment and frame sides. To make these cuts, set up a 3⁄4"-wide (19mm) dado along with a rabbet fence. Set the height of the blade to 3⁄4" (19mm) and adjust the fence to expose slightly more than 1⁄8" (3mm) of the blade. Mark the table at the front and the back of the blade so you can see where to start (or stop) the cut. Mark the front side of each pediment piece 9" (23cm) from the mitered end to show where the rabbets stop.

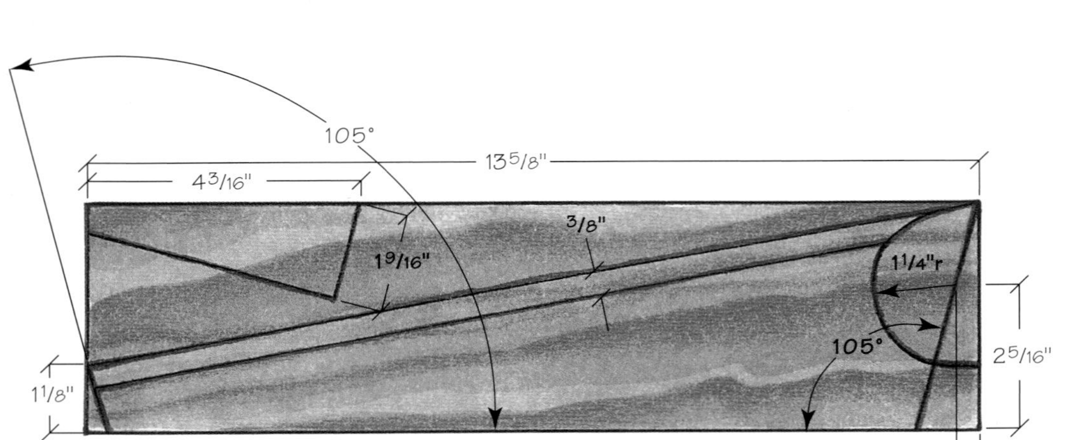

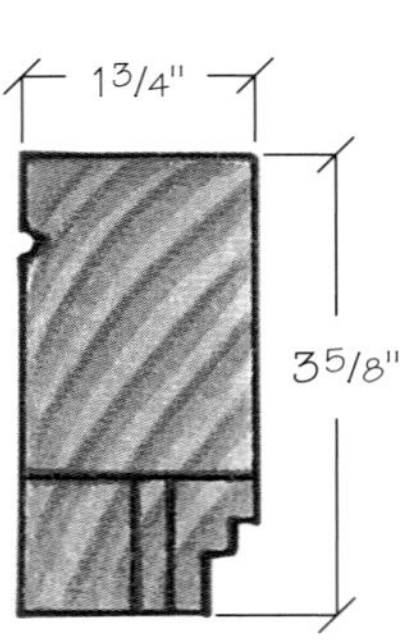

[11] PIVOT THE PEDIMENT

For one of the pediment pieces, you'll need to pivot the piece onto the spinning blade. Lower the blade beneath the table. Position the piece with the mark aligned with the mark towards the rear of the table. Clamp a stop block behind the piece to prevent kickback. Raise the blade to its original height. Hold the piece against the fence above the blade. Start the saw and slowly pivot the piece down into the cut. When the piece is down on the table, push it past the blade to complete the cut.

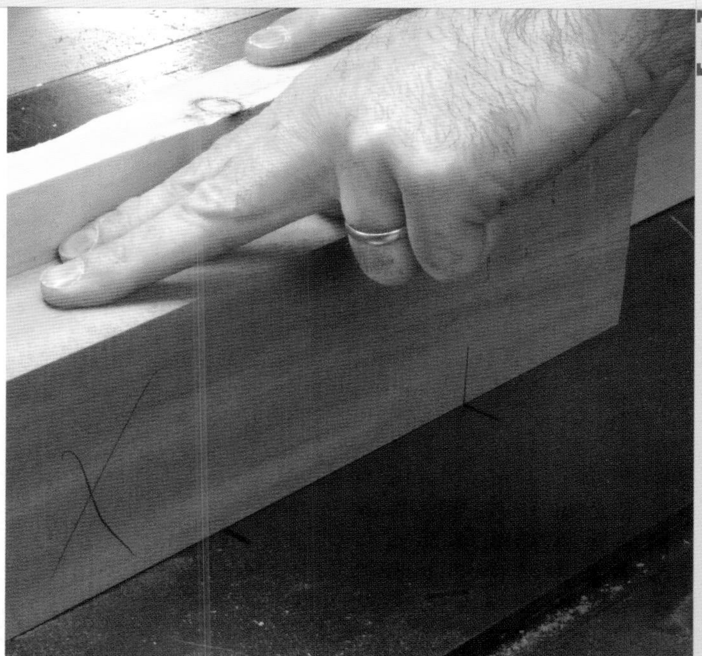

[12] CUT THE SECOND PIECE

For the second piece, cut as you would normally but stop when the line on the piece reaches the line toward the front of the table. Also cut rabbets along the inside edges of the frame sides. These cuts should stop 2½" (63mm) from the upper ends of the pieces. Reset the fence and the blade height to make a second rabbet. This one should be ½" (13mm) wide (blade height) and ¼" (6mm) deep [the exposed blade width should be slightly more than ⅜" (9mm)]. Re-mark the table and make the second rabbets in all the pieces.

[13] GLUE THE PIECES TOGETHER

Cut notches in the top edges of the pediment pieces. Cut a spline to fit into the slots you just cut into the ends of the pieces—the grain in the spline should run perpendicular to the glue line. Apply glue to the joint and clamp the pieces together.

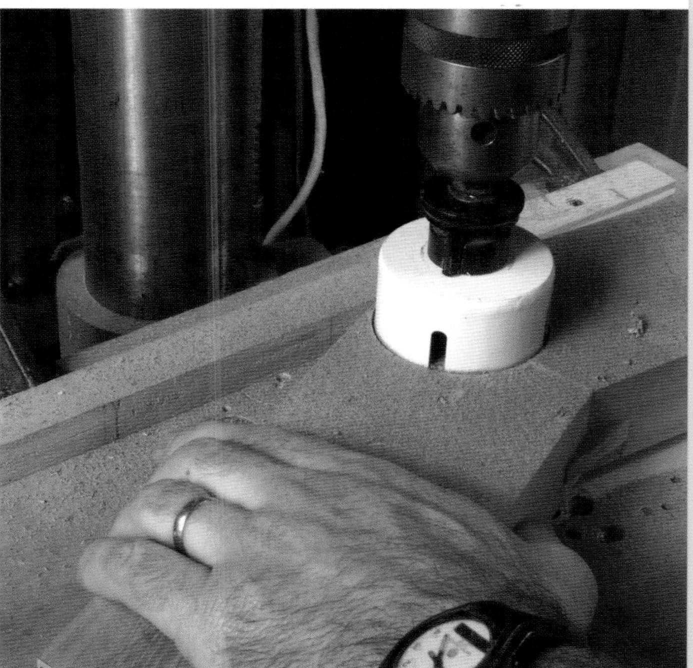

[14] DRILL THE ROUND DETAIL

Chuck a 2½" (63mm) Forstner bit (or a hole saw) in your drill press. Carefully locate the center of the circular cutout and drill the pediment assembly. Sand the inside of the cutout to clean it up.

[15] TAPER THE PEDIMENT

Lay out the taper along the top edge of both sides of the pediment. Place the pediment on a carrier board so that one of the layout lines is aligned with the edge of the carrier board. Screw a fence to the carrier board to hold the pediment in this position. Position the rip fence so the blade runs along the edge of the carrier board. Hold the pediment in place and run the carrier board along the fence to make the cut. Flip the pediment over to cut the second side.

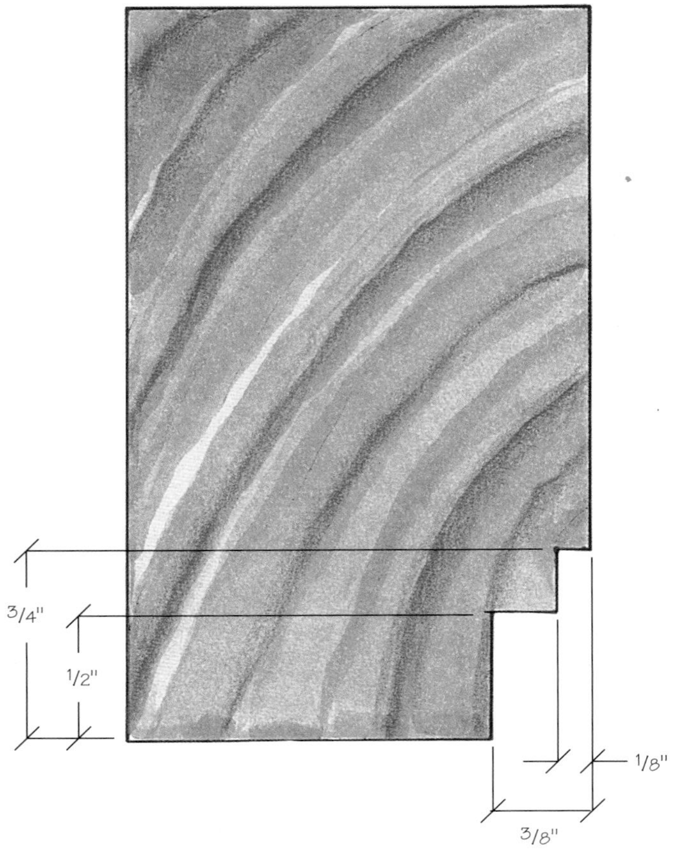

[16] BEAD THE PEDIMENT

Put the molding head back on the saw with the V-cutter. Make a V-cut along the top edge of the pediment. Place the cut into the circular cutout on each side.

[17] CUT THE ENDS OF THE PEDIMENT

Cut off the ends of the pediment at 86°.

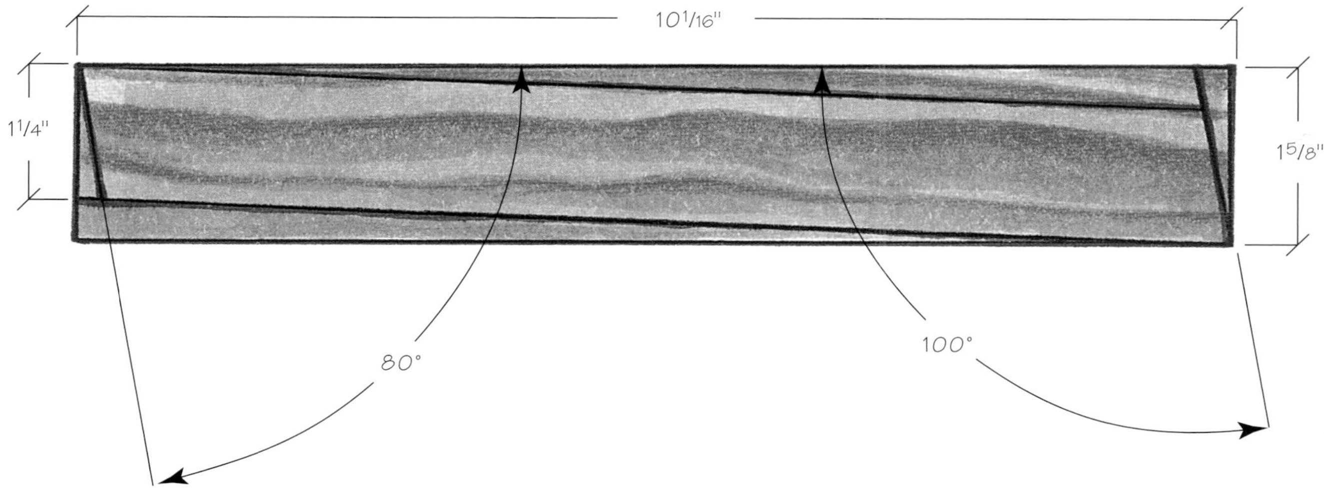

[18] TAPER THE FRAME BOTTOMS

Cut the pieces for the frame bottom to the size listed. Crosscut one end of each piece at 79° and slot the pieces for a spline as you did for the pediment pieces. Be sure to mark the outside faces so you can keep track of them. Lay out the tapers on the pieces and cut them with the aid of a carrier board as you did before. Note: This time you're tapering the pieces before gluing them together.

[19] CHAMFER THE FRAME BOTTOM

To chamfer the top outside corner of the frame bottom pieces, tilt the blade at a 45° angle. Position one of the pieces against the fence with its outside face toward the blade, its bottom side down and its narrower end toward the blade. Adjust the fence so the blade just nicks the upper corner of the piece. Note: On a saw that tilts to the left, the fence should be to the left of the blade. Push the piece through the cut. The chamfer should go from next to nothing at the narrow end to about ½" (13mm) wide at the wide end. Repeat with the second piece, this time running the wide end first.

[20] GLUE THE FRAME BOTTOM
Cut off the narrow ends of the pieces at an 80° angle. Glue wedge-shaped clamping blocks to the undersides of the pieces. Insert the spline and glue the pieces together. Once the glue dries, cut off the wedges.

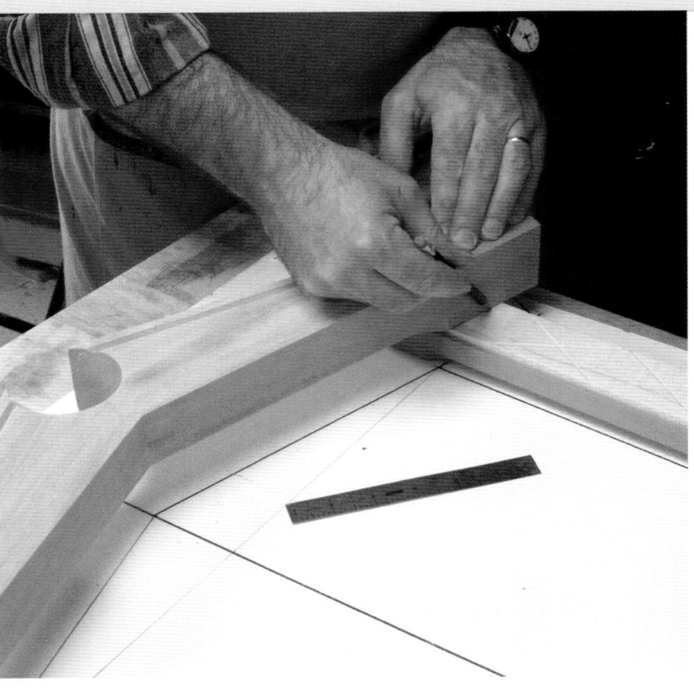

[21] MARK THE FRAME SIDES
Set up the frame side pieces on your full-size drawing, carefully aligning them with the layout. Place the pediment on top of the sides. Even if it doesn't quite agree with the drawing, be sure to position it "square" to the center line. Mark the frame sides where the pediment crosses. Repeat the process with the frame bottom.

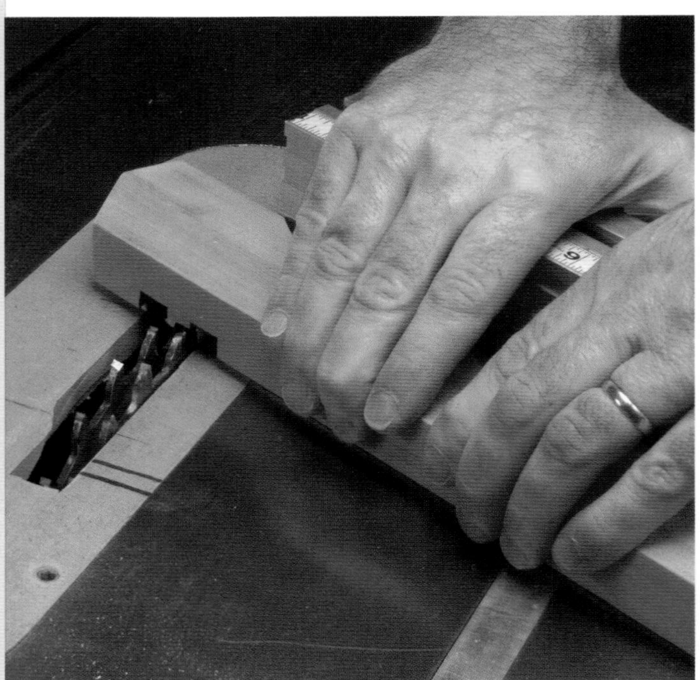

[22] CUT NOTCHES ACROSS THE FRAME SIDES
Set up a $^1/_2$"-wide (13mm) dado blade and set it to make a $^1/_2$"-deep (13mm) cut. Cut notches which will receive the pediment and bottom across the frame sides. You'll need to reset the angle on the miter gauge to accommodate the taper of the pieces.

[23] MARK THE PEDIMENT FROM THE BACK SIDE
Assemble the frame on the drawing, with the pieces set firmly in their notches. Flip over the frame to mark the bottom and pediment for their notches. Reset the height of the dado blade to match the remaining side thickness. Cut the notches in the bottom and pediment.

[24] NOTCH THE FRAME BOTTOM

Slip the frame bottom into its notches in the side pieces. Mark the rabbets on the bottom. Set up a wide dado and make repeated passes to cut away a place for the mirror and its backing to run past.

[25] PAINT THE LINES

Apply a coat of finish to seal the surface and keep the paint from wicking into places it shouldn't go. Paint the lines with artists' acrylic paint. The blue in the photo is a mix of ultramarine blue and phthalocyanine green. Cut the mirror backing to size and paint its bottom edge with the same color.

[26] SQUARE THE RABBETS

Glue the frame together. Square the rabbets with a chisel where the pediment meets the sides. Cut a piece of hardboard to serve as a pattern for the mirror. Take the pattern to the glass shop and have them cut a piece of 1/4" (6mm) mirror to match. Have them grind the bottom edges as they will be exposed.

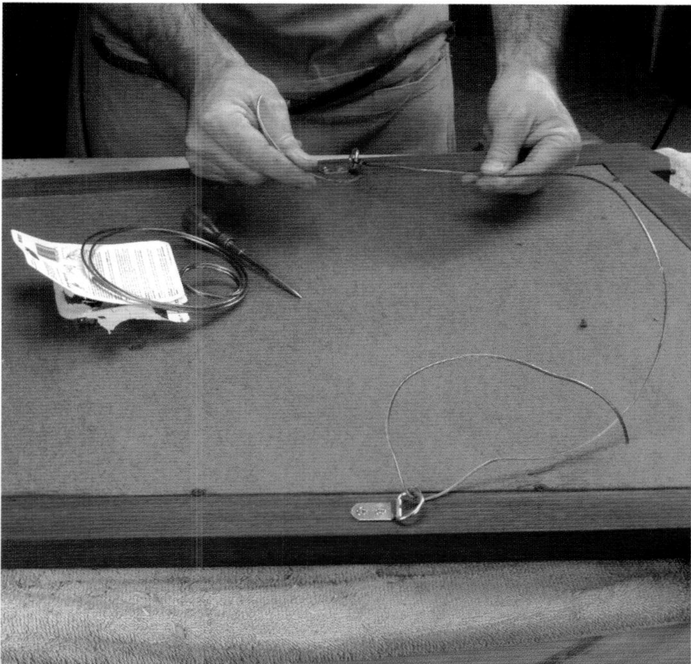

[27] SCREW THE SCREW EYES IN PLACE

Sand and finish the frame. Note: Be sure to clean up and finish rabbets that will be in contact with the glass—you'll be able to see them in the mirror. Set the mirror in place along with the backing. Screw the backing to the frame every 8" (20cm) or so. Also install screw eyes and a heavy-duty wire for hanging.

OCCASIONAL TABLE [7]

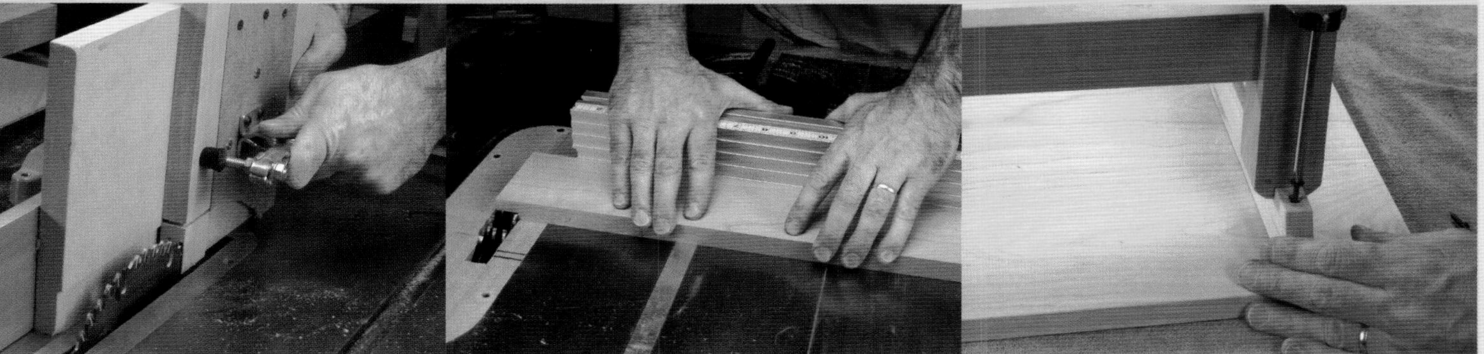

A lot of woodworking and practicality are built into this little stand. As shown, it's a great occasional table that you can use in the living room as a tall end table, in the kitchen to hold your microwave, or even on the sun porch as a plant stand. It can also work in conjunction with the bookstand (page 48) as an excellent stand-up desk. Try it in your foyer as a place to open and sort the mail, or in your office as a place to work while you pace back and forth puzzling out an idea.

From a woodworking perspective, the stand presents several challenges. This first thing you may notice is that the ends of the tenons are exposed. This type of joint is known as a through-tenon. Exposed joinery requires extra effort because you can't really hide your mistakes.

A second, related challenge is in the way the mortises are cut. When I started designing the projects for this book, I realized that there were some operations the table saw just couldn't do—drilling holes and cutting mortises among them. The trick is to cut the mortices from the inside out. Sounds crazy, but it works.

Start by cutting two pieces for each leg—each piece is slightly more than half the thickness of the final leg. Dado the pieces to create the mortises. Then glue them face to face with spacers in the dadoes to maintain alignment. After the glue dries, cut the pieces in half again and dado the resulting pieces to create the second set of mortises. Even if you don't build this stand, it's worth reading through the project to learn how to make the mortises. Who knows, you may find a use for the technique some day.

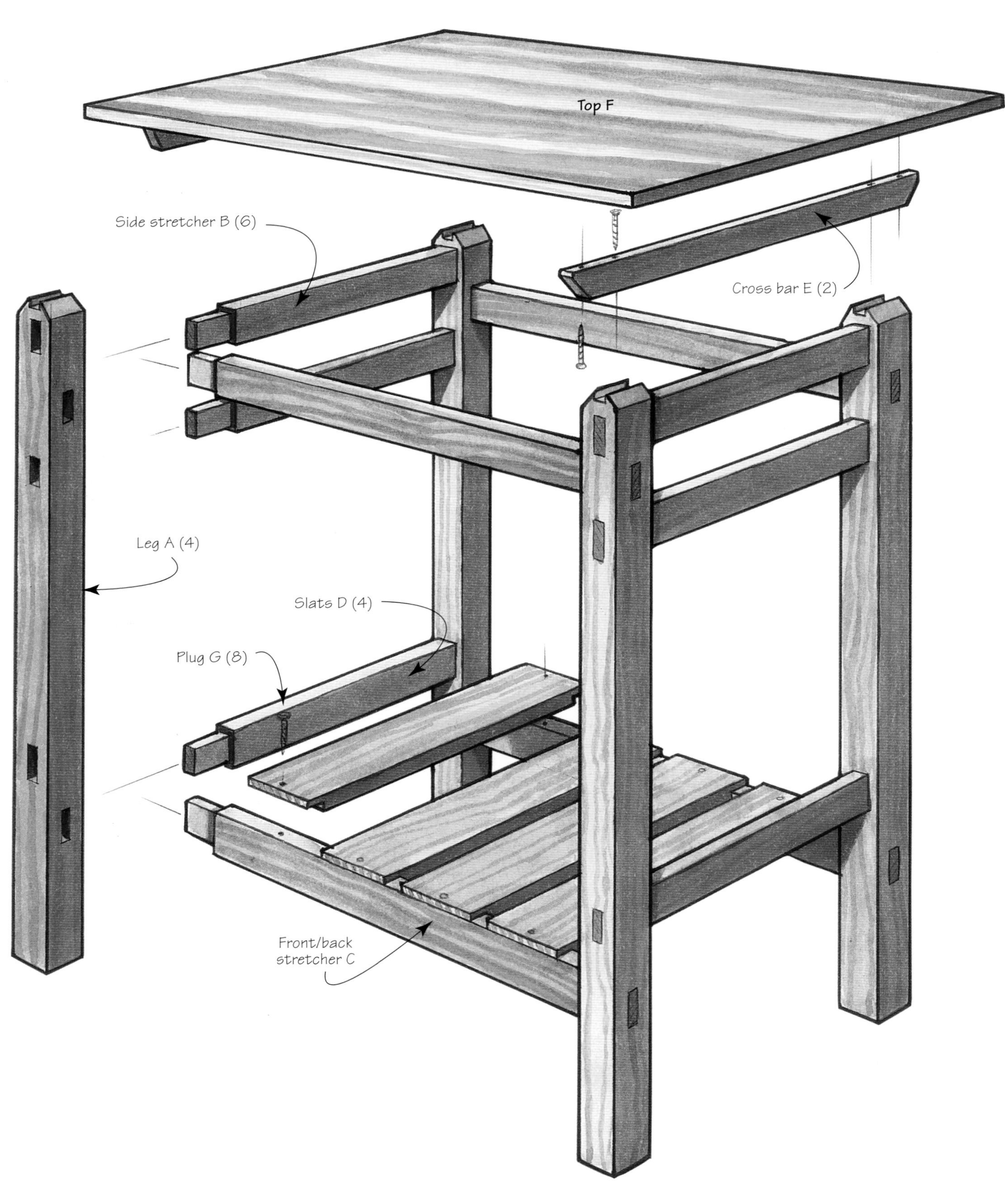
Top F
Side stretcher B (6)
Cross bar E (2)
Leg A (4)
Slats D (4)
Plug G (8)
Front/back
stretcher C

[TABLE] inches (millimeters)

REFERENCE	QUANTITY	PART	STOCK	THICKNESS	(mm)	WIDTH	(mm)	LENGTH	(mm)	COMMENTS
A	4	legs	hardwood	1 9/16	(40)	1 9/16	(40)	32 1/4	(819)	
B	6	side stretchers	hardwood	3/4	(19)	1 1/2	(38)	18	(457)	
C	4	front/back stretchers	hardwood	3/4	(19)	1 3/4	(44)	23	(584)	
D	4	slats	hardwood	3/4	(19)	3 1/2	(89)	17 1/4	(438)	
E	2	cross bars	hardwood	5/8	(19)	1 1/2	(38)	21 1/4	(540)	
F	1	top	hardwood	3/4	(19)	22	(559)	27 1/2	(698)	
G	8	plugs	hardwood							3/8 (9mm) diameter

[HARDWARE]

4	10" × 2 1/2" (25cm × 6cm) Screws
4	8" × 2" (20cm × 5cm) Screws
8	8" × 1 1/4" (20cm × 3cm) Screws

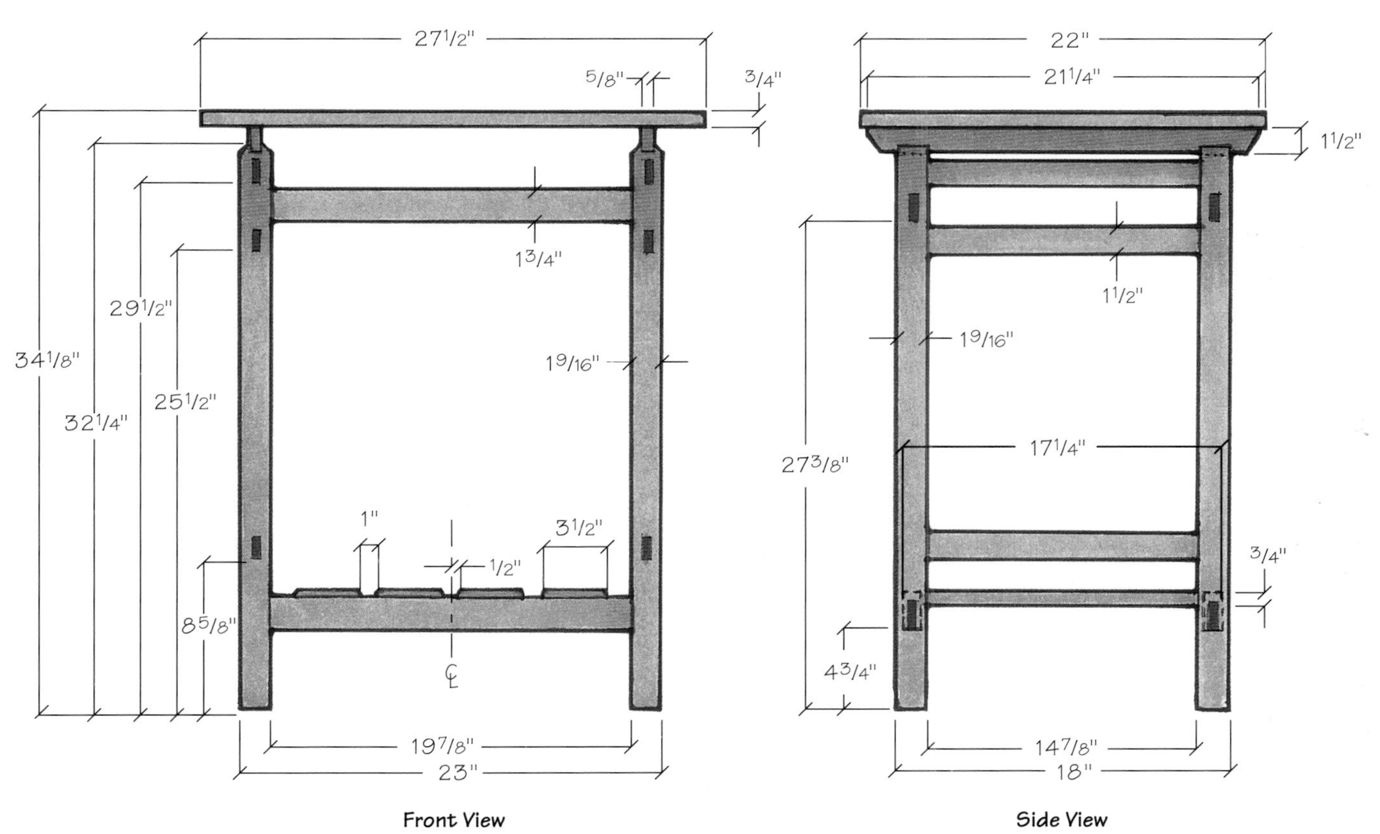

Front View

Side View

[1] CUT THE DADO

Cut the pieces for the legs to size. If possible, use 5/4 stock so you'll have a little extra thickness to play with as insurance. Set up a $^3/_4$"-wide (19mm) dado, and adjust its height to $^1/_4$" (6mm). Lay out the dadoes for the side stretchers on one of the pieces. Set up a stop on your miter gauge fence to align the top of the mortise with the right side of the dado blade. Make the cut on all eight pieces with their bottom end against the stop.

[2] MAKE THE SECOND CUT

Make the dado wider by inserting a $^1/_2$" (13mm) spacer between the bottom end of the leg and the stop. I used $^1/_2$" (13mm) MDF for the spacer, but you can use pretty much anything. The exact thickness doesn't matter, as long as you use the same spacer for each set of cuts.

Using Spacers

Why use a spacer to set the size of a mortise when you could just as easily move the stop? The answer is consistency. When you use the stop to locate the first cut of each mortise, you are ensuring that the mortise location will be the same on each leg. Then, when you use the spacer for the second cut, you are ensuring that each mortise will be the same size, even when you reset the stop for the second and third stretchers. In contrast, if you were to use only the stop for the second cut on each group of mortises, it is likely that the mortise size would vary a little from setup to setup. This in turn means the tenons would have to vary as well. If you use the spacer, all the mortises will be the same and you can cut all the tenons with the same setup.

[3] GLUE THE LEGS

To finish the mortises, glue the pieces to each other. Before applying the glue, cut pieces of scrap to use as space holders. These pieces should fit snugly in the dadoes. Wrap the space holders with plastic packing tape to prevent them from sticking to the glue. Note: The best way to do this is to select scrap pieces that fit snugly, then take one swipe off each side with a block plane and wrap with tape. Spread glue on the mating surface and clamp the pieces together.

[4] RIP THE LEG IN HALF

When the glue dries, scrape away any squeeze-out. Trim the edges by running the pieces through the saw with the saw set just slightly less than the overall width of the piece. Turn the piece around, bump the fence over and trim the second side. Reset the fence and rip the legs right down the middle to prepare them for the second set of mortises.

[5] DADO THE SECOND MORTISE

Lay out the locations of the mortises for the front and back stretchers. Cut the dadoes the same way you did earlier, using a stop to locate the cut and a spacer to control its width. This time, however, use a 3/4" (19mm) stop to make the cut slightly wider. Make the cuts on all eight pieces. Glue the pieces together. Make a second set of spacers for the new mortises, and use the original spacers through the first set.

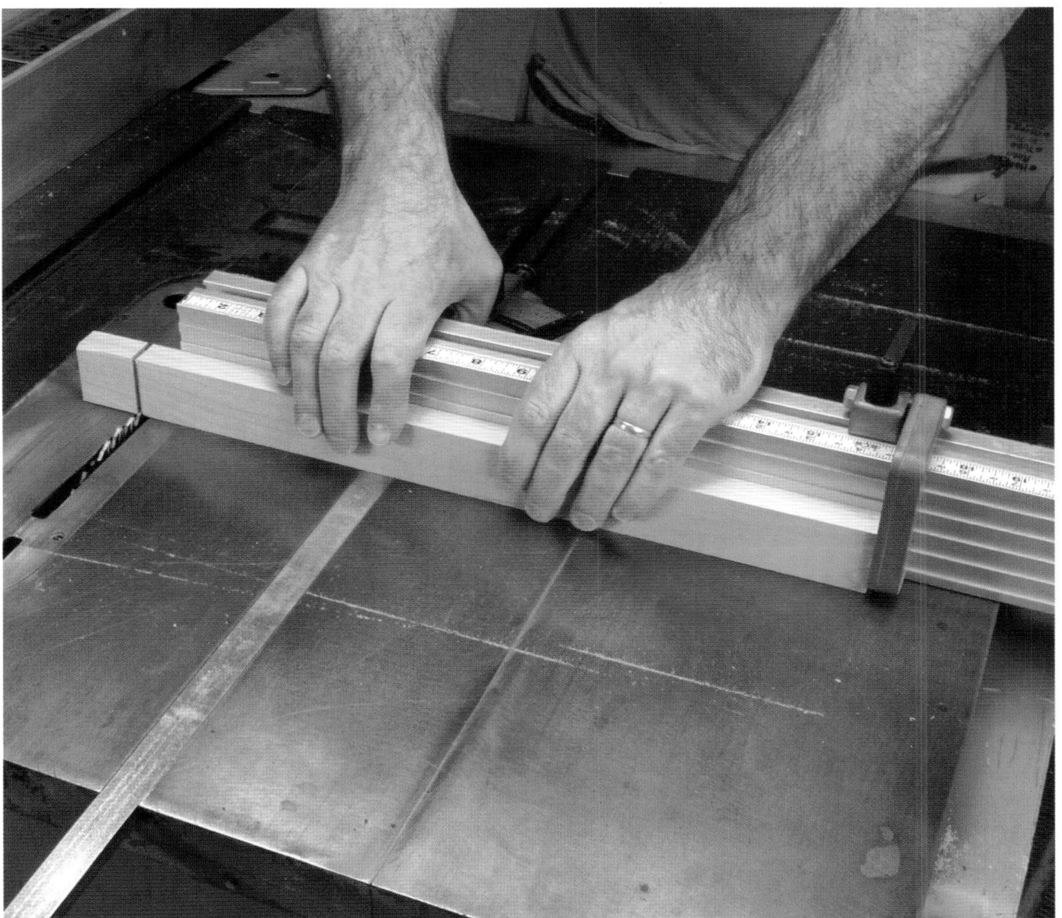

[6] MAKE THE SHOULDER CUTS

When the glue dries, cut the legs to their final width and thickness of 1 9/16" (40mm), keeping the mortises centered across the width of the pieces. Set up a regular saw blade to make the shoulder cuts for the tenons on the stretchers. Adjust the height of the blade to 1/8" (3mm). Use a stop to control the location of the cut as you guide the pieces across the saw with the miter gauge. The length of the tenons should be just short of 1 9/16" (40mm). Make the cut on all four sides of each side stretcher. (You'll repeat the process with the front and back stretchers, but because the mortises were cut with a different setup, it is safer to cut the tenons on the front and back stretchers separately.)

[7] MAKE THE FIRST CHEEK CUT
Make the cheek cuts with the help of a simple tenoning jig. Start by setting the blade height just shy of the shoulder created where the pieces are standing on end. Adjust the rip fence to position the piece for the first cut. This cut should remove approximately 1⁄8" (3mm) of material.

[8] CUT THE SECOND CHEEK
Bump the fence over to make the second cheek cut. Start by making the tenon too big, then adjust the fence slightly to sneak up on the right setting.

Dynamite Glue-Spreading Technique

When it comes to spreading glue across a surface, it's hard to beat a printer's brayer. These hard rubber rollers are commonly available at most arts and craft stores. Look in the print-making aisle.

[9] MAKE THE SIDE CUTS

Mark the width of the tenon on the face of one of the pieces. Make the first side cut, holding the piece against the jig. Turn the piece around and make the second cut with the same setting. Again, start with a setting that cuts the pieces too big, then make small adjustments until the size is just right. Repeat the process to cut tenons on the front and back stretchers.

[10] CUT NOTCHES ON THE LEGS

Set up a $^{5}/_{8}$-wide (16mm) dado blade and set the depth of cut at $^{3}/_{8}$" (9mm). Cut notches in the top of the legs by guiding the pieces through the cut with the simple tenoning jig. Be sure to orient the legs with the mortises for the side stretchers facing forward (and back). The notches should be centered across the width of the piece. Note: If you are making this as a base for the bookstand, dry assemble it first and clamp everything together. Then place the bookstand on top of the legs so you can mark them for the notch locations.

[11] CHAMFER THE TOPS OF THE LEGS

Switch back to a regular saw blade and tilt it to 45°. Chamfer the top corners of the legs that are parallel to the notches. Guide the pieces through the cut with the miter gauge. Note: On my left-tilt saw, I set up the miter gauge to the right of the blade with a fence that extended past the blade to the left. Clamp a stop block to the fence to control the location of the cut.

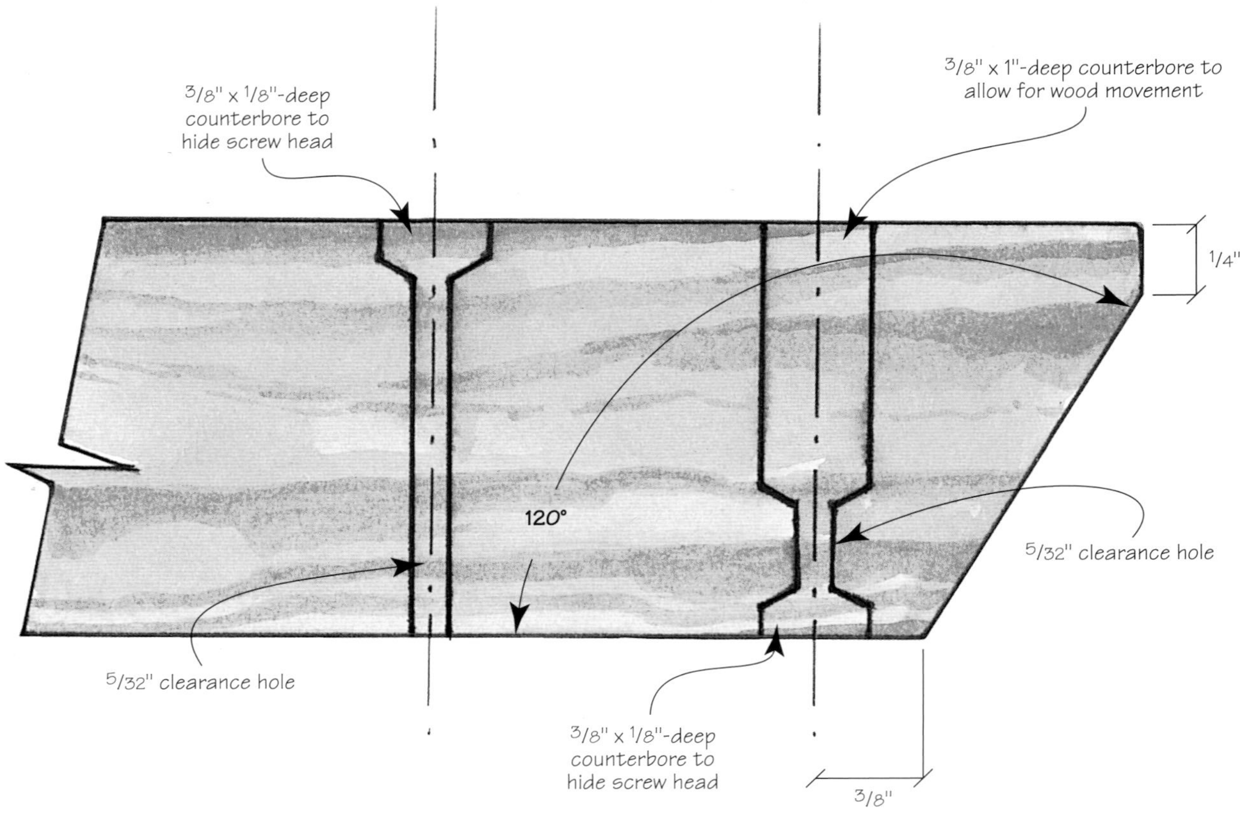

[12] RABBET THE SLATS

Practice assembling the pieces to check the fit of the joints and trim piecess as needed, then apply glue to the joints and clamp the pieces together. Cut the slats to size and rabbet them to fit in between the front and back stretchers. Make the rabbets about 5⁄16" (8mm) deep. Use a stop on the miter gauge fence to maintain consistency.

[13] CUT THE END OF THE CROSS BAR

Cut the cross bars to the size listed. Set your miter gauge to 120° to the blade. Cut both ends of each cross bar at this angle, leaving an approximately 1⁄4" (6mm) flat at the top of each piece. Also drill holes through the cross bars for mounting. Note that the holes for attaching the top are oversized to allow for seasonal wood movement. Screw the cross bars to the legs with 2 1⁄2" (3mm) screws.

[14] ATTACH BASE TO TOP

Edge-glue boards to make up a panel for the top. Cut the panel to size. Place it upside down on your bench with the base inverted on top of it. I use an old towel as a pad to protect sanded surfaces. Measure carefully to center the base on the top. Screw the base in place with 2" (51mm) screws.

[15] DRILL FOR DOWELS

If you are going to place the bookstand on the base, drill $^1/_4$" (6mm) holes in the tops of the legs for short lengths of dowel. Use dowel centers to transfer the locations to the underside of the bookstand. Drill matching holes in the bookstand. Glue pieces of $^1/_4$" (6mm) dowel in the holes in the legs. These will serve to keep the stand in place, but they will also allow you to remove the stand easily for moving or storage.

[16] INSTALL THE SLATS

Drill the ends of the slats for screws and counterbore them for $^3/_8$" (9mm) plugs. Center a 1" (25mm) spacer on the front and back stretchers and clamp it in place. Screw slats to the stretchers on either side of the spacer with $1^1/_4$" (32mm) screws. Reposition the spacer to aid in placing the third and fourth slats, and screw the slats in place. Plug the holes. When the glue dries, sand the plugs flush with the surface. Finish the table with your favorite wood finish. I used several coats of wiping varnish on the piece in the photo.

ENTERTAINMENT CENTER [8]

For those raised on Gameboys and Play Station 2s, this entertainment center might seem a bit tame. Rather than accommodating for the latest plasma screen or sub-woofer, its shelves are sized for board games such as Scrabble and Monopoly. It was made to sit humbly in a room, waiting for a rainy Sunday afternoon when the power goes out and those high-priced gadgets become null and void. You might also institute a monthly un-plugged family game night in an effort to rediscover how much fun it is to sit and talk and play games that aren't electronically enhanced.

The piece offers several wood-working challenges. The case itself is fairly straight for-ward—tongues on the horizontals fit into dadoes cut across the sides. If you choose to paint the case, you can screw these pieces together and plug the holes to hasten construc-tion. The face frame is beaded, and the beads are mitered at the corners where the stiles and rails come together.

The doors are out of the ordinary; in fact, they have become one of my signature details. The rails and the outer stiles are tapered for a more dynamic look than a simple rectangular frame can provide. The panel features a cove-cut bevel that creates the raised field. The door pulls complement the doors' subtle angles and curves.

The entertainment sham is made of poplar and painted with a green milk paint, then fin-ished with several coats of wiping varnish. The doors and the top are made of cherry and also received a clear wiping varnish finish.

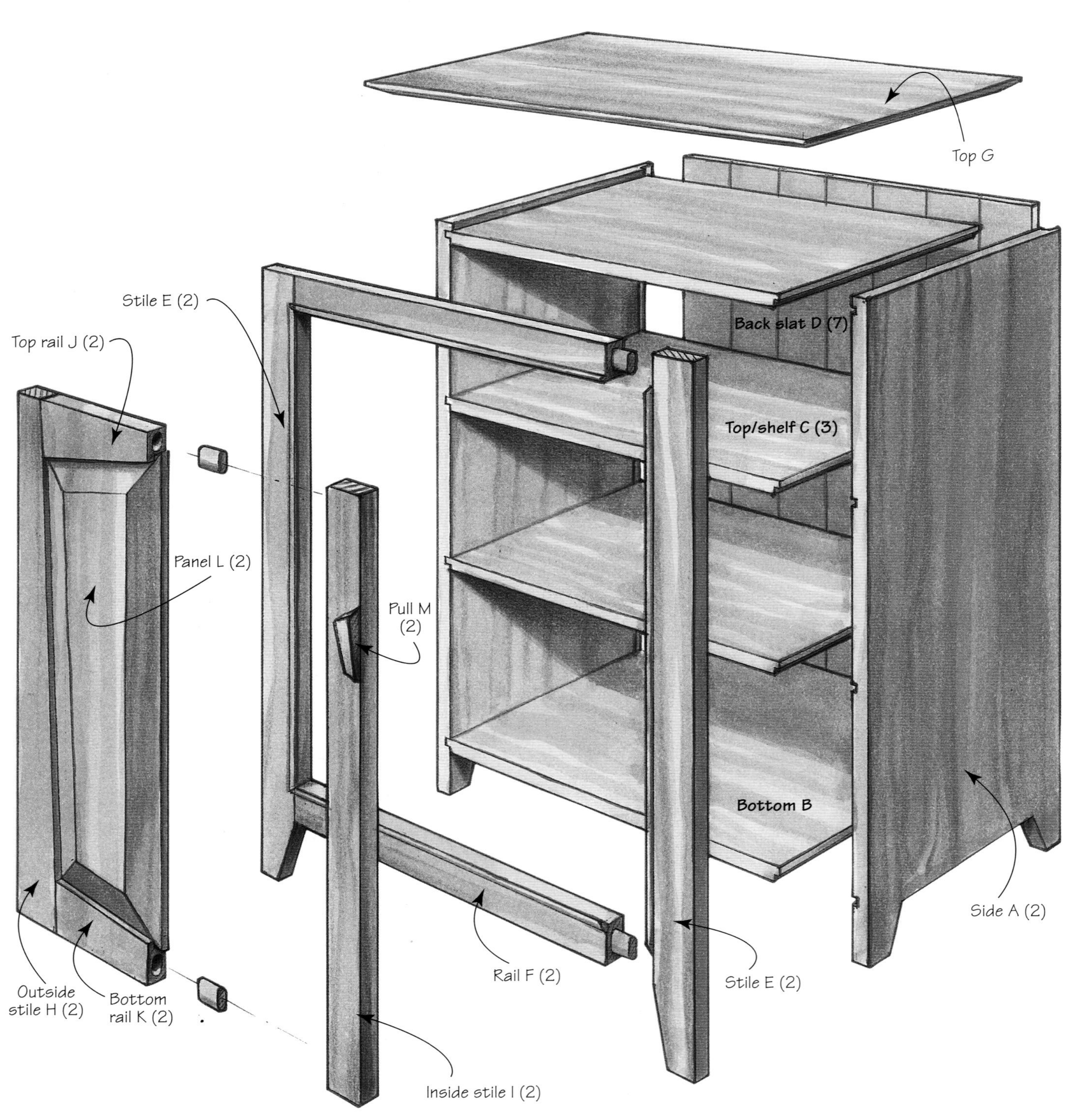
Top G
Back slat D (7)
Top/shelf C (3)
Bottom B
Side A (2)
Stile E (2)
Top rail J (2)
Panel L (2)
Pull M
(2)
Rail F (2)
Stile E (2)
Outside
stile H (2)
Bottom
rail K (2)
Inside stile I (2)

[CASE] inches (millimeters)

REFERENCE	QUANTITY	PART	STOCK	THICKNESS	(mm)	WIDTH	(mm)	LENGTH	(mm)	COMMENTS
A	2	sides	hardwood	$3/4$	(19)	14	(356)	37	(940)	Paint-grade
B	1	bottom	hardwood	$3/4$	(19)	14	(356)	24	(610)	Paint-grade
C	3	top/shelves	hardwood	$3/4$	(19)	$13 1/2$	(342)	24	(610)	Paint-grade
D	7	back slats	hardwood	$1/2$	(13)	4	(102)	$34 1/4$	(876)	Paint-grade
E	2	stiles	hardwood	1	(25)	2	(51)	37	(940)	Paint-grade
F	2	rails	hardwood	1	(25)	$1 1/2$	(38)	$23 1/2$	(597)	Paint-grade
G	1	top	hardwood	$5/8$	(16)	$17 1/4$	(438)	$29 1/2$	(749)	Clear finish

[DOORS]

REFERENCE	QUANTITY	PART	STOCK	THICKNESS	(mm)	WIDTH	(mm)	LENGTH	(mm)	COMMENTS
H	2	outside stiles	hardwood	1	(25)	$2 5/8$	(66)	$31 1/2$	(800)	
I	2	inside stiles	hardwood	1	(25)	$1 1/2$	(38)	$31 1/2$	(800)	
J	2	top rails	hardwood	1	(25)	$2 3/4$	(67)	$7 5/8$	(194)	
K	2	bottom rails	hardwood	1	(25)	3	(76)	$6 5/8$	(168)	
L	2	panels	hardwood	$5/8$	(16)	8	(203)	28	(711)	
M	2	pulls	hardwood	1	(25)	$1 1/16$	(27)	$5 1/4$	(133)	

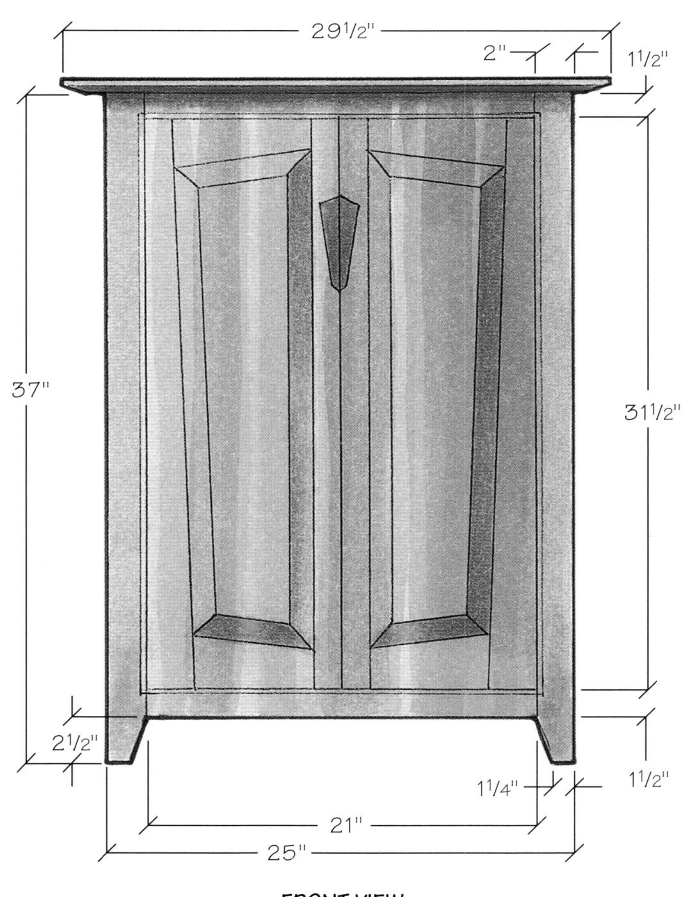

FRONT VIEW

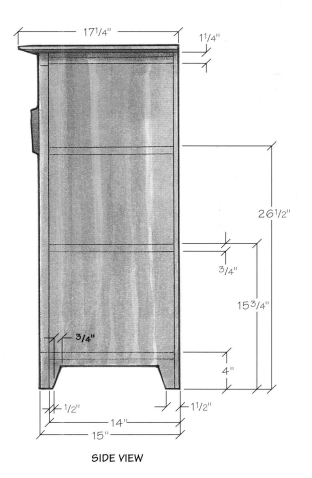

SIDE VIEW

Flat Panels

When making a project that involves wide glued-up panels, find a commercial shop that will run your pieces through their wide belt (or drum) sander. These machines make short work of flattening glue lines and getting the pieces to a uniform thickness and flatness. It is well worth the money you'll spend to have the pieces sanded for you.

[1] CUT THE DADOS ACROSS THE SIDES

Cut the sides of the case to size. You'll probably have to edge-glue narrower pieces to make up the wider widths. Make sure the panels are flat, then cut the dadoes across the sides for the top, bottom and shelves. The dados should be $^1/_2$" (13mm) wide and $^1/_4$" (6mm) deep.

[2] CUT THE TONGUES ON THE PANELS

Lower the dado blade a hair. Cut the tongues on the ends of the top, bottom and shelves by running the pieces past the blade on end. If this feels awkward, attach a piece of plywood to your fence to extend its height. Start by cutting one of the tongues slightly too wide, then bump the fence over and recut. Repeat the process until the pieces go together with firm hand pressure. Cutting the tongues this way helps ensure that they end up a consistent thickness.

[3] RABBET FOR THE BACK

While the dado blade is set up, cut rabbets in the sides and bottom for the back slats. The rabbets should be $^1/_2$" (13mm) wide and $^1/_2$" (13mm) deep.

[4] MARK THE FENCE FOR THE BACK OF THE BLADE

Put a crosscut or combination blade on the saw and raise it to its highest position. Move the fence so it's close to the blade. Mark the fence to indicate where the blade meets the table at both its leading and trailing edges.

[5] LAY OUT THE FOOT CUTS

Lay out the foot cuts on the bottom ends of both sides. Make additional layout lines to transfer the location of the upper ends of the angled feet to the ends of the pieces as shown.

[6] MAKE THE FOOT CUTS

Set the fence so it measures $2^1/_2$" (6cm) to the outside of the blade. Lower the blade beneath the saw table. Position one of the sides with its bottom edge against the fence and the away transfer line aligned with the away blade line on the fence. Hold the piece securely, start the saw and raise the blade to its highest point. I am comfortable making this cut alone, but you can get help if it feels at all awkward. Slowly push the piece along the fence until the near transfer line aligns with the near blade line on the fence. Lower the blade and stop the saw. Repeat the process with the second side.

[7] FINISH THE CUTS WITH A HAND SAW

Even with the blade at its highest setting, the end of the kerf it leaves won't be vertical. So you'll still have to finish the cuts with a handsaw (or a jigsaw). While you're trimming the pieces, also saw along the angled layout lines to complete the foot cutouts.

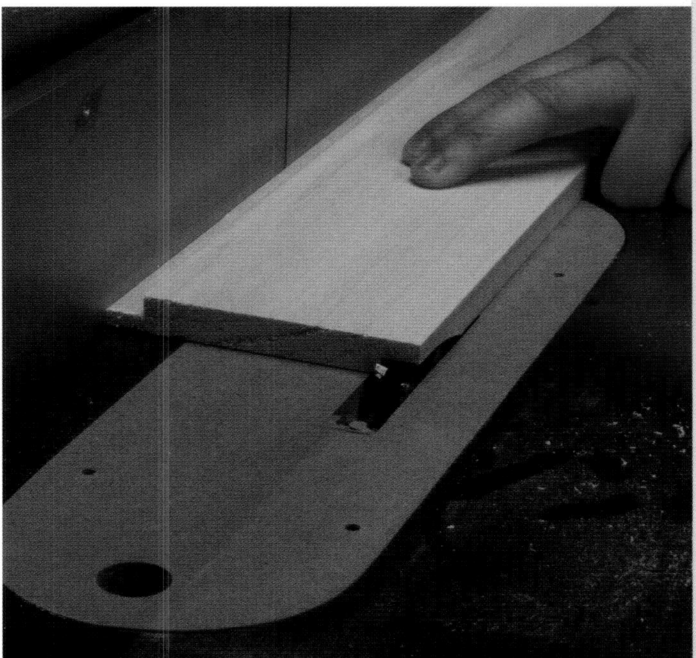

[8] RABBET THE BACK SLATS

Cut the back slats to size. Set up your dado head and rabbet the edges of the slats. The five center slats are rabbeted on both edges, while the two outer slats are rabbeted only on one edge. The rabbets should be $^1/_2$" (13mm) wide and $^1/_4$" (6mm) deep.

[9] ASSEMBLE THE CASE

Brush glue into the dadoes and assemble the case. If you are going to paint the case, you can use finish nails or screws to clamp everything together. Putty or plug the holes later. If you plan to use a stain or clear finish, forgo the fasteners in favor of clamps and cauls. Be sure to measure the diagonals to make sure the case is square.

[10] PLACE THE BACK SLATS

Turn the case face down on your assembly table. Starting at one side, set the back slats in place and fasten them in place with 3D finish nails. Predrill the holes to avoid splitting the wood. Nail the outer slats to the sides as well as to the top, bottom and shelves. This will help keep the case from racking. The center slats require two nails in each of the horizontal members spaced about 5⁄8" (16mm) on either side of center. Leave a little space [about 1⁄16" (1mm)] between the slats to allow room for expansion.

[11] BEAD THE FACE FRAME

Cut the face frame's rails and stiles to size. While you're at it, also cut the doors' stiles and rails roughly to size so their thickness matches that of the face frame. Set up a moulding head and cut a bead along one edge of each piece. (You can also do this on a router table with a beading bit.)

[12] MORTISING STILES

There aren't many things you cannot do on a table saw, but cutting mortises is one of them. These days, one of the quickest, best ways to cut mortises is with a plunge router. Make a jig to hold the pieces as you rout. Center the mortises across the thickness of the stiles and locate them.

[13] CUT THE SHOULDERS OF THE TENONS

Lay out the tenons on the ends of the rails, using the mortises in the stiles as a guide. Set the height of the blade to make the shoulder cuts. Place a stop block against the rip fence and use it to control the length of the tenons. Make the shoulder cuts by guiding the rails through the cut with the miter gauge. Be sure to make shoulder cuts in a test piece that you'll use when you're setting up to make the cheek cuts.

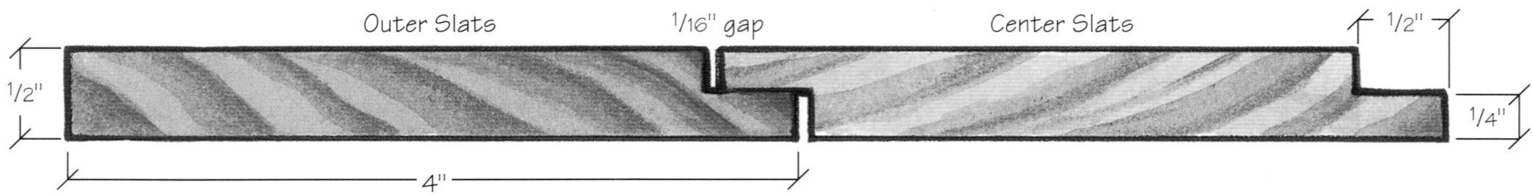

[14] CUT THE EDGE SHOULDERS
While you have the stop block and miter gauge set up, raise the blade and make the shoulder cuts as well.

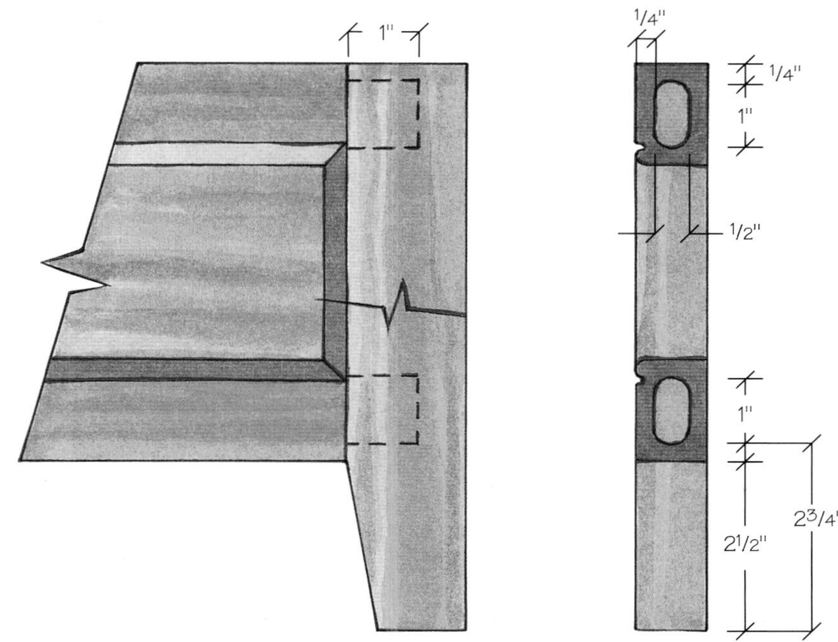

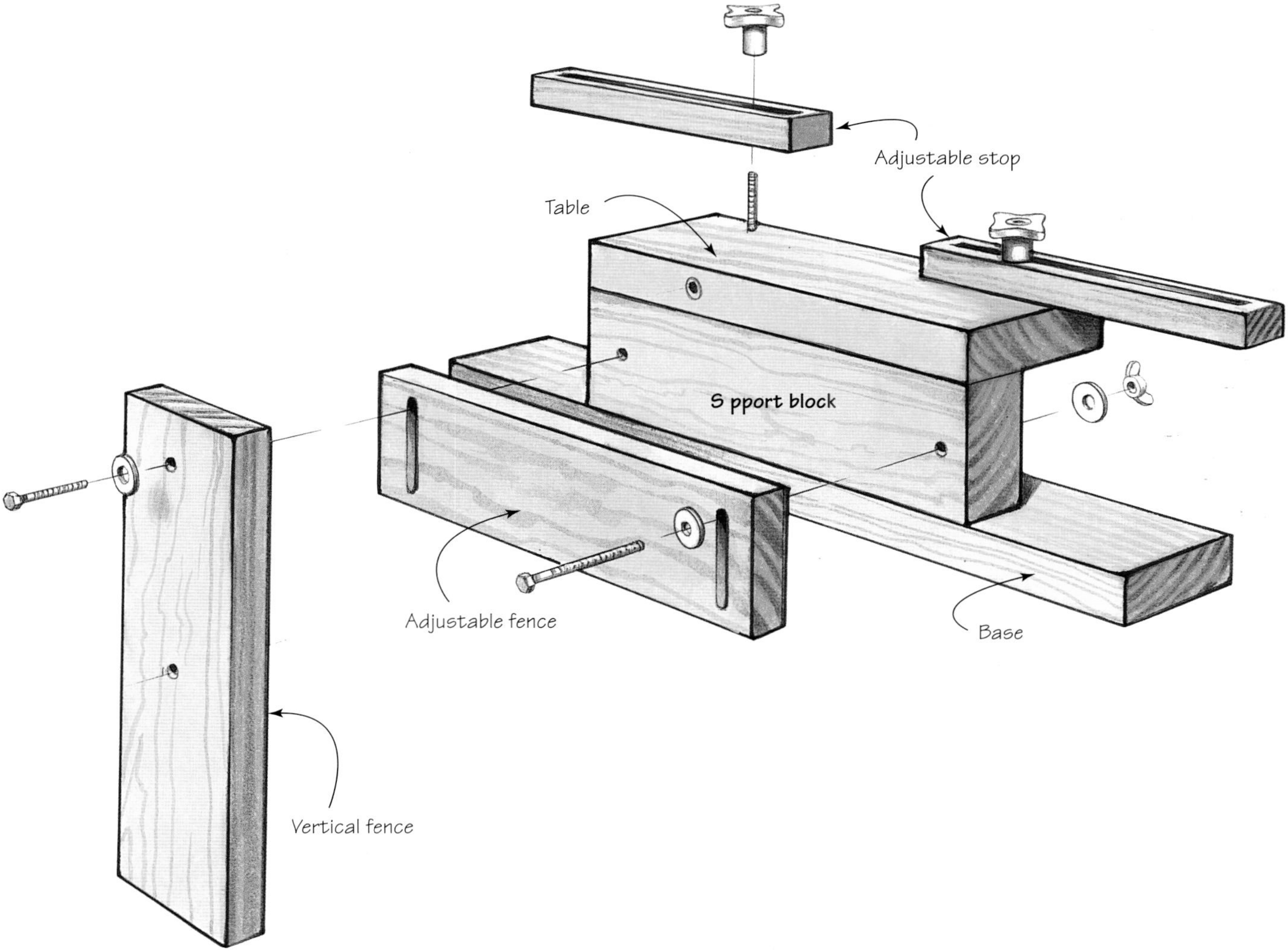

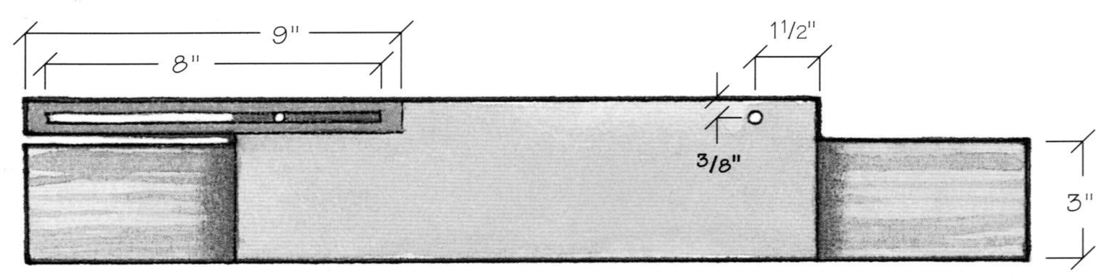

TOP VIEW

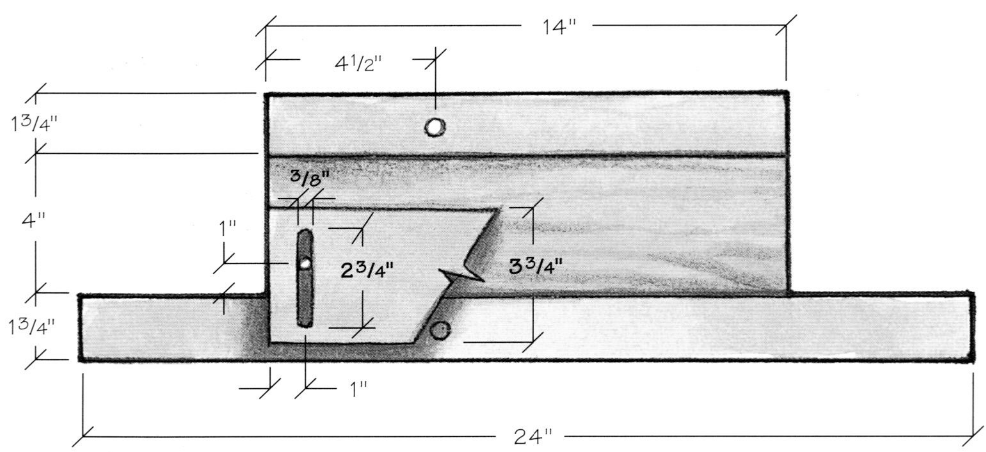

FRONT VIEW

VERTICAL FENCE

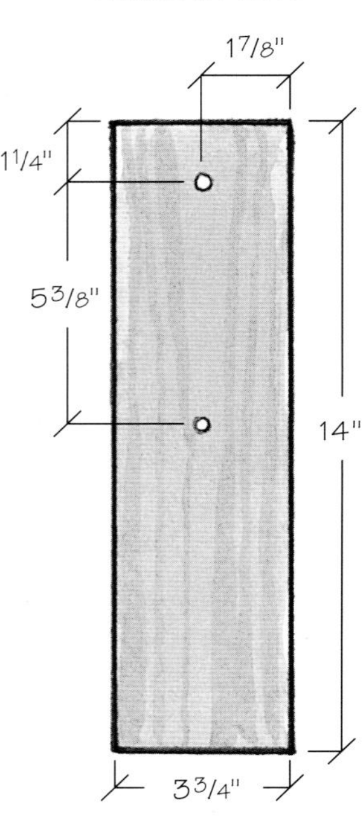

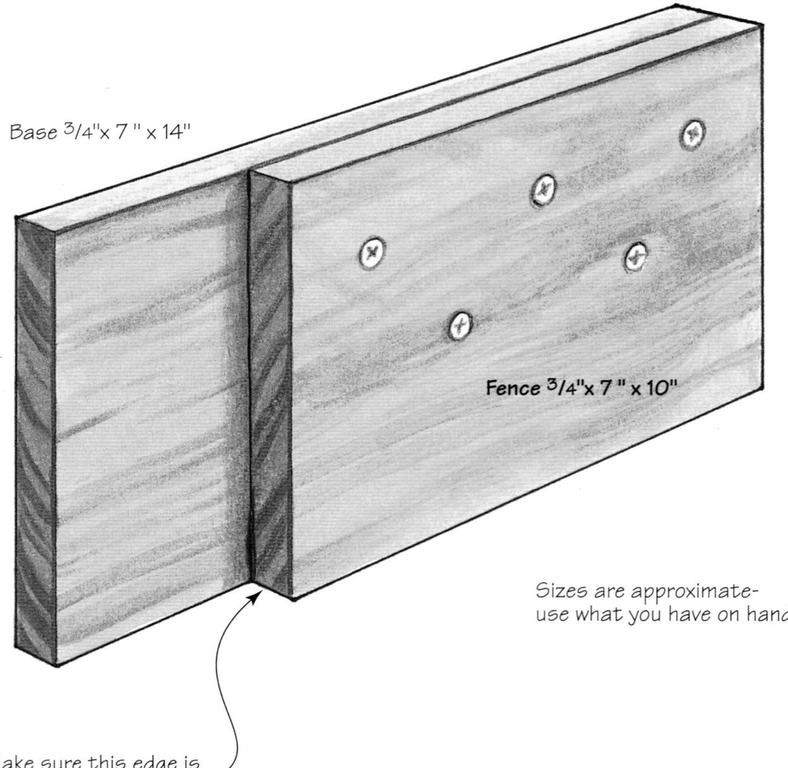

[15] MAKE THE INSIDE CHEEK CUT
Adjust the blade height to make the cheek cuts. Clamp the test piece in the simple tenoning jig, then adjust the rip fence to position the jig to make the inside cheek cut. Make the cut and hold the test piece up to one of the mortises for comparison. Make adjustments as needed, then make the inside cuts on all the rail pieces. (Load the pieces into the jig with the beaded side out for consistency).

[16] MAKE THE OUTSIDE CHEEK CUT
Move the fence away from the blade to set up for the outside cheek cuts. Clamp the test piece back in the jig. Lock the fence in position and make a test cut—ideally the tenon will be too wide. Bump the fence over and cut again. Repeat until the tenon slides into the mortise with firm hand pressure. Make the second cheek cuts in the rest of the rails.

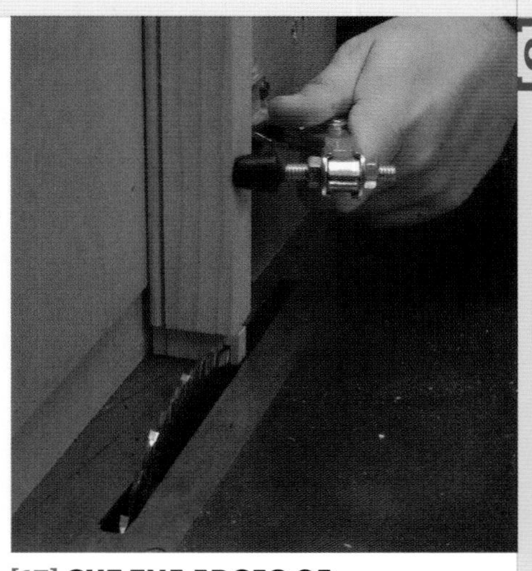

[17] CUT THE EDGES OF THE TENONS
As a final step to cutting the tenons, hold the pieces perpendicular to the jig's fence and make the edge cuts. Round the corners of the tenons with a file.

[18] MAKE THE MITER CUTS ON THE BEADS ON THE RAILS
Tilt the blade to a 45° angle and adjust its height so it barely cuts through the bead on the edges of the frame pieces. Hold the rails on edge against the miter gauge, and miter the bead at either end.

[19] MITER THE STILES
While you have the blade tilted, also miter the beads on the stiles. Slip the rails in to their mortises so you can mark where the stiles should be cut. Make the cuts, using the miter gauge to guide the pieces past the blade.

[20] CUT THE BEAD
After making the miter cuts on the stile beads, you'll need to cut away the excess bead so the frame pieces can mate correctly. Adjust the blade so it is square to the table. Raise it to its highest setting—this makes the end of the saw kerf as perpendicular to the table as possible. Mark the saw table and the fence to show the limit of the cut as you did in step four. Also mark both the front and the back of the stiles to show where the cuts should stop. Set the rip fence so the cut removes the bead. Run each end of the stiles along the fence until the layout line aligns with the mark on the fence. Carefully back the piece out of the cut.

[21] FINISH THE CUT

Finish the cuts with a handsaw, then clean up the freshly sawn surfaces with a sharp chisel.

[22] MAKE THE TAPER CUT ON THE STILES

Lay out the angled cut on the bottom end of one of the stiles. Place the stile on a carrier board with the layout line aligned with the board's edge. Screw a fence and a stop to the board to help hold the stile in position. Adjust the rip fence so the blade will cut right along the edge of the carrier board. Hold the stile atop the carrier and slide the pieces through the cut. Repeat with the second stile.

[23] CLAMP THE FACE FRAME TO THE CASE

Glue the face frame together. When the glue dries, glue the frame to the front of the case. Trim the edges of the face frame flush with the sides of the case.

[24] TAPER THE DOOR STILE

Cut the stiles and rails for the doors to the sizes listed in the materials list. Lay out the taper on one of the door stiles. Align the layout line with the edge of a carrier board. Screw a fence and a stop to the carrier to help hold the stile in place. Adjust the rip fence so the blade cuts along the edge of the carrier board, then make the tapered cut. Repeat with the second stile.

[25] CUT THE ANGLE ON THE END OF ONE OF THE RAILS

Taper the rails the same way you tapered the stiles. Cut the wider ends of the rails to an angle that matches the taper of the stiles. Roughly assemble the two door frames so you can look at the grain patterns. When you have an arrangement you like, mark the frame pieces with the cabinetmaker's traditional triangular marks.

[26] CUT THE GROOVES IN THE STILES
Set up a $^5/_{16}$" (8mm) wide dado and set its height to $^3/_8$" (9mm). Cut grooves along the inside edges of all the door frame pieces. Switch back to a regular saw blade, and cut filler pieces to fill in the grooves at the ends of the stiles. Glue the filler pieces in place.

[27] MORTISING THE END OF A RAIL
Because of the angles and the sequence of assembly involved, the door frames are put together with loose tenons. In a loose tenon joint, both pieces are mortised and a separate "loose" tenon is fit in between. Cut the mortises in the ends of the rails by holding the pieces vertically in the mortising jig. Cut the mortises in the stiles as you cut them in the face frame pieces.

[28] GLUE UP A DOOR FRAME (C-SHAPED)
Cut a strip of tenon stock to fit in the mortises. Round over the corners, then cut the individual tenons to length. Glue the rails to the tapered stiles. Don't worry about damaging the other ends of the rails—I purposefully left them long, and we will trim them later. Be careful that the pieces go together flat—a twisted door frame is difficult to hang correctly.

[29] TRIM THE DOOR FRAME
After the glue dries, trim the inside ends of the rails to their final length. (Check this by measuring the inside opening in the face frame.) This cut ensures that the ends of the rails are colinear. Because of the taper on the outside rail, if you tried to assemble the frame all at once, those ends probably would not line up and the frame would not go together correctly.

[30] TRACE A DOOR FRAME ONTO A PANEL
Assemble the door frames and trace the openings onto the door panels. Draw a line $^5/_{16}$" (8mm) outside the traced line to indicate the actual panel size. Cut the panels to size.

[31] COVE THE DOOR PANELS

Set up for a cove cut (actually half a cove) that is $1\frac{1}{2}$" (38mm) wide and $5\frac{1}{15}$"-inches (129mm) deep. Cove the edges of the panels by running the pieces along the angled fence. Note: You'll get a cleaner cut if you use a bullnose molding cutter rather than a regular saw blade to make the cut. Also note that you should make the cut in several shallow passes.

[32] PIN THE PANEL

Sand the panels and give them at least one coat of finish. Slip them into the frames, and check to make sure there is a little room for expansion from side to side. Glue the inside stiles in place. On the back of each door, drill $\frac{1}{8}$" (3mm) holes through the rails for pins that will hold the panels in place and prevent them from rattling. Center the holes along the rails about $\frac{1}{4}$" (6mm) from the inside edge.

[33] MORTISE THE HINGES

Cut the mortises for the hinges in both the sides of the door frames and the sides of the face frame. You can do this by hand with a sharp chisel, but I find it easier to make up a C-shaped template to use with a router.

[34] BEVEL THE TOP

Cut the top to size. Tip the blade to a 79° angle and bevel its ends and front edge. Screw the top in place, driving the screws up from inside the case.

[35] INSTALL THE PULLS

Make up the pulls for the doors (see "Making the Pulls" on page 93). Remove the top and doors from the case. Paint the case, then finish everything with several coats of clear finish. Reassemble everything and screw the pulls in place. Add the catches to the underside of the upper shelf and the back of the doors to finish the piece.

Making the Pulls

The pulls for the Entertainment Center each require a series of four tapered/beveled cuts. Unfortunately, because the pulls are mirror images of each other, most of the cuts require their own setup. I made a sled that includes fences for all the different setups. While this may seem like a lot of work for making two door pulls, you may be surprised where else these pulls can be used. Once you have the sled, it's easy to make another set of pulls for a different project.

[1] MARK THE BLANKS
Cut the pulls to size 1" × 1$^{1}/_{16}$" × 5$^{1}/_{4}$" (25mm × 27mm × 133mm). Set the pieces side by side to experiment with the grain match. When you have a match you like, mark the mating sides and the outside faces.

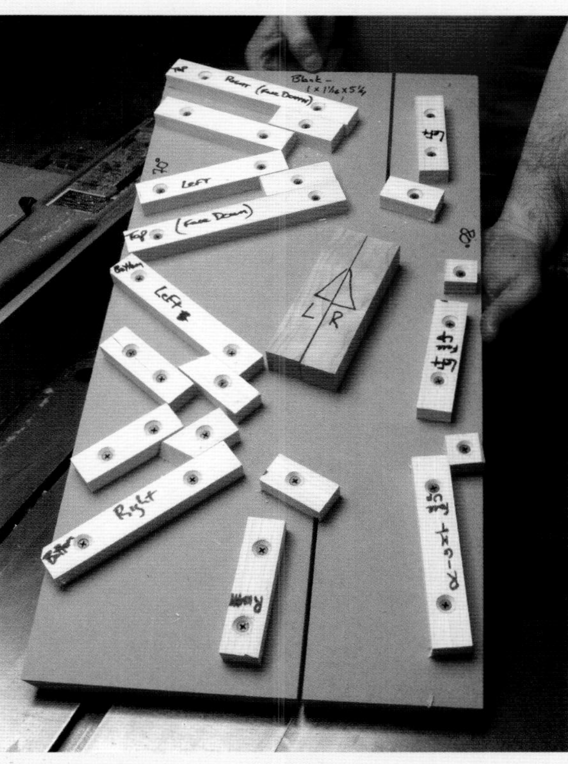

[2] MARK THE JIG
When I make a jig like this, I write key information right on the jig. This helps down the road when I want to reuse it. Mark the various fences so you can tell how to orient the pieces. I also save a blank pull as well as a finished pull with the jig as samples.

[3] MAKE THE FIRST CUT
Tilt the blade to 82°. Note: If your saw tilts to the right, you should make up the sled as a mirror image of the one in the diagram and make the cuts with the fence to the left of the blade. Adjust the rip fence so the blade runs along the beveled edge of the jig. With the outside face up, load the left pull blank in the first slot and make the cut, beveling the top end of the pull. Then load the right blank in the second slot and cut it.

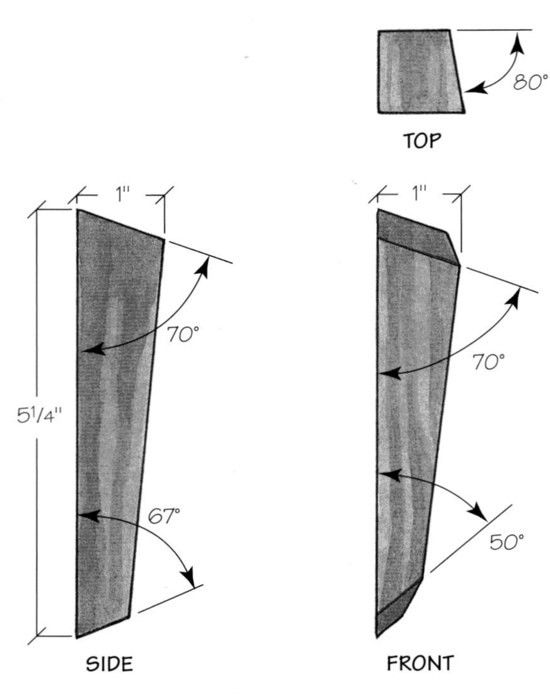

[4] MAKE THE SECOND CUT

Turn the pieces over (marked face down) and make the second cuts, beveling the bottom end of the pull. Use the third (left pull) and fourth (right pull) slots in the jig for these cuts.

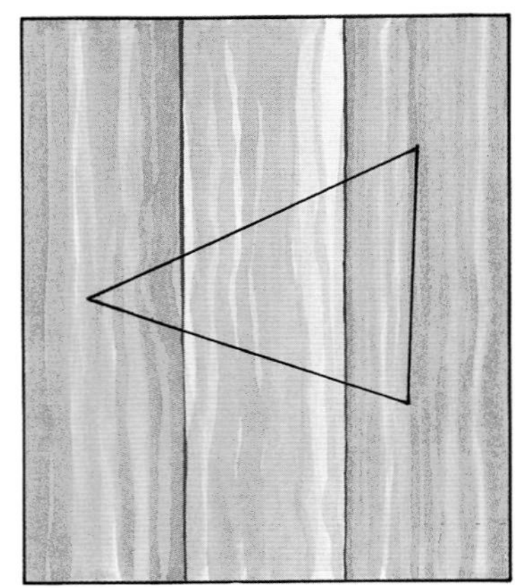

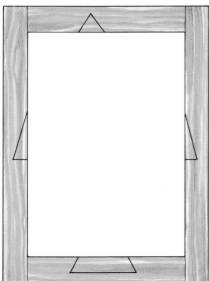

When you're arranging boards to be edge-glued (upper drawing at left), draw a big triangle across all the pieces when you have the grain arranged the way you want it. You can easily put the pieces back in order after jointing, etc.

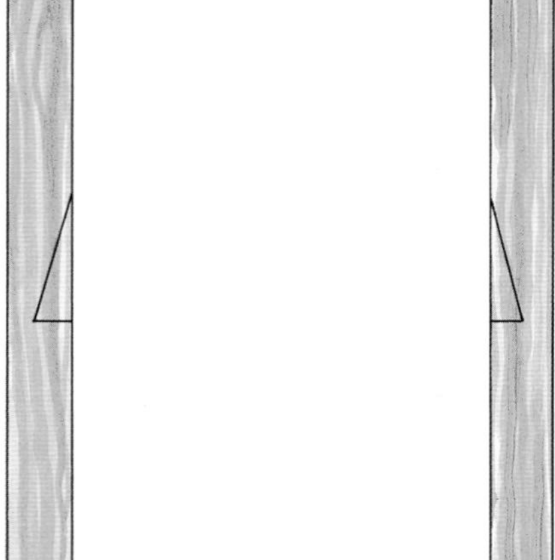

When arranging pieces for a frame (lower drawing at left), mark each part of the assembly with a partial triangle as shown. The top rail gets the top of the triangle, the bottom rail gets the bottom of the triangle and the stiles each get their respective side of the triangle. The open part of the triangle indicates the inside edge of the piece and the triangle itself shows the orientation of the piece.

If you are making more than one frame (drawing above), add a number inside each of the marks. Or, add a letter — L for the left door, R for the right, etc. If you want to keep track of two adjoining stiles (if they were cut from a single board, for example) draw a triangle across them both.

[5] MAKE THE THIRD CUT

Make the third cut for both pieces with the fifth slot. Adjust the blade to make it square to the table. Move the rip fence so the blade cuts along the edge of the jig. Load each piece in the jig with its outside face out and the bottom end toward the blade.

[6] MAKE THE FOURTH CUT

Turn the jig around and tilt the blade back to 82°. Cut the left pull using the sixth slot. The outside face (freshly tapered) should be up, and the bottom end of the pull should be toward the blade. Cut the right pull using the seventh slot. Again, the outside face should be up, but this time the top end should be toward the blade.

87°

7°

108°

70°

50°

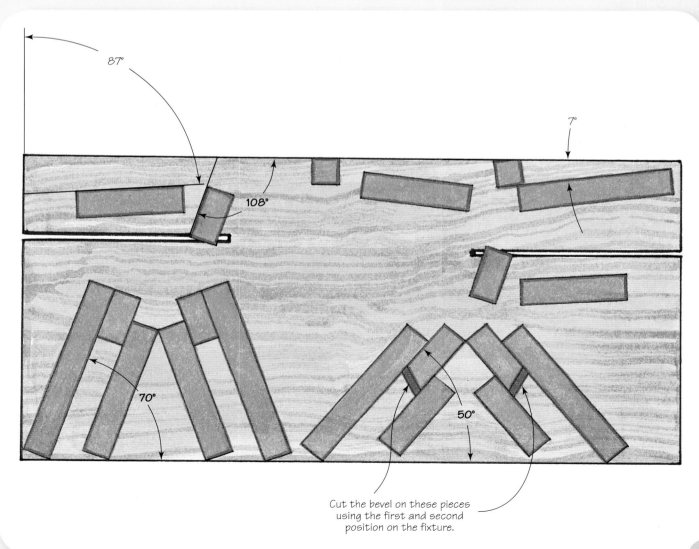

Cut the bevel on these pieces using the first and second position on the fixture.

CYLINDRICAL CHEST OF DRAWERS [9]

Furniture that's made on the table saw has to be straight, right? Not necessarily. While it's true that the saw excels at cutting straight lines, it is capable of the occasional curve. Case in point: this cylindrical chest of drawers. It was made almost entirely on the saw, curves and all. How to do it involves a jig or two, some careful layout and clever subterfuge.

The jigs allow you to make the curved cuts, and the careful layout shows you where those cuts are to be made. The subterfuge comes from the fact that the cylindrical part of the case isn't really cylindrical, it only appears to be. In actuality, the case is a polygon made up of flat staves. The staves are attached at the top and bottom to two faceted pieces of plywood that help maintain the angles between the pieces. The only parts that are truly curved are the top and bottom. All of these pieces are cut on the saw.

The drawers are joined at the corners with half-blind finger joints and housed in an inner case made of plywood. The finished chest in the photo is made of jatoba (a South American hardwood) with wenge accents and maple drawers. For the how-to photos, I used white oak for the case, sycamore for the drawers and walnut for the accents to make a second chest.

As a warning, this piece is probably the most demanding in the book. The tricky part is cutting the faceted plywood disks. The layout for the disks isn't particularly difficult; you just need to be fussy about getting it right. Then you need to be very careful as you align the pieces on the saw to make the cuts.

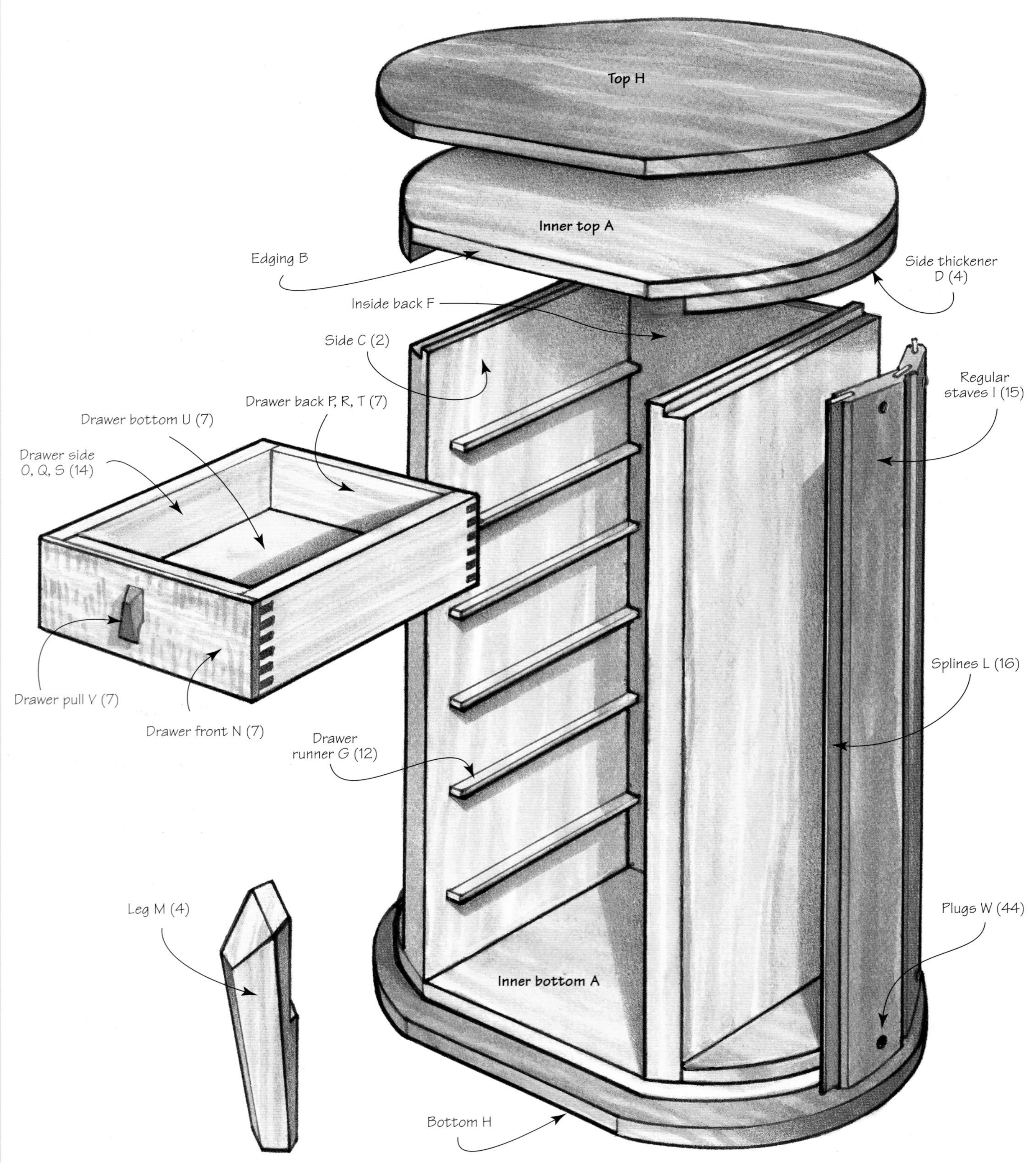

Front trim K (2) is applied to the front staves J (2).

[CASE] inches (millimeters)

REFERENCE	QUANTITY	PART	STOCK	THICKNESS	(mm)	WIDTH	(mm)	LENGTH	(mm)	COMMENTS
A	2	inner top/bottom	plywood	1/2	(13)	12 3/4	(324)	14 1/2	(368)	Cut 5 1/2 (140mm) long for side thickeners
B	2	edging	hardwood	1/8	(3)	9/16	(14)	14 1/2	(368)	Contrasting accent color
C	2	sides	plywood	3/4	(19)	10 1/2	(267)	22 1/8	(562)	
D	4	side thickeners	plywood	1/2	(13)	12 3/4	(324)	2 1/2	(63)	Cut from ends of inner top/bottom
E	2	back thickeners	plywood	1/2	(13)	2 1/8	(54)	9 1/2	(241)	Leave long and cut to fit
F	1	inside back	plywood	1/4	(6)	8 1/2	(216)	21 1/4	(540)	
G	12	drawer runners	hardwood	1/4	(6)	1/2	(13)	10	(254)	
H	2	top/bottom	hardwood	5/8	(16)	14 1/4	(362)	15 3/8	(9)	
I	15	regular staves	hardwood	9/16	(14)	2 1/8	(54)	22 3/4	(578)	
J	2	front staves	hardwood	9/16	(14)	2	(51)	22 3/4	(578)	
K	2	front trim	hardwood	9/16	(14)	9/16	(14)	22 3/4	(578)	Contrasting accent color
L	16	splines	hardwood	1/8	(3)	7/8	(22)	21 3/4	(552)	Dye with an eye-catching color
M	4	legs	hardwood	1 1/2	(38)	1 5/8	(41)	6 1/4	(159)	
N	7	drawer fronts	hardwood	3/4	(19)	3 1/4	(82)	8	(203)	Resaw to create half-blind finger joints
O	2	top drawer sides	hardwood	3/8	(9)	2 1/2	(63)	10	(254)	
P	1	top drawer back	hardwood	3/8	(9)	2 1/2	(63)	8	(203)	
Q	10	regular drawer sides	hardwood	3/8	(9)	3	(76)	10	(254)	
R	5	regular drawer backs	hardwood	3/8	(9)	3	(76)	8	(203)	
S	2	bottom drawer sides	hardwood	3/8	(9)	2 3/4	(70)	10	(254)	
T	1	bottom drawer back	hardwood	3/8	(9)	2 3/4	(70)	8	(203)	
U	7	drawer bottoms	plywood	1/8	(3)	9 5/8	(244)	7 1/2	(190)	
V	7	drawer pulls	hardwood	1/2	(13)	1/2	(13)	1 1/2	(190)	
W	44	plugs	hardwood							5/16 (8mm) diameter; contrasting accent color

[HARDWARE]

6	#8 × 1 1/2" (40mm) Roundhead Screws
2	#8 × 1" (25mm) Roundhead Screws
40	#6 × 1 1/4" (30mm) screws
4	#6 × 2 1/2" (65mm) screws
7	#4 × 3/4" (20mm) screws

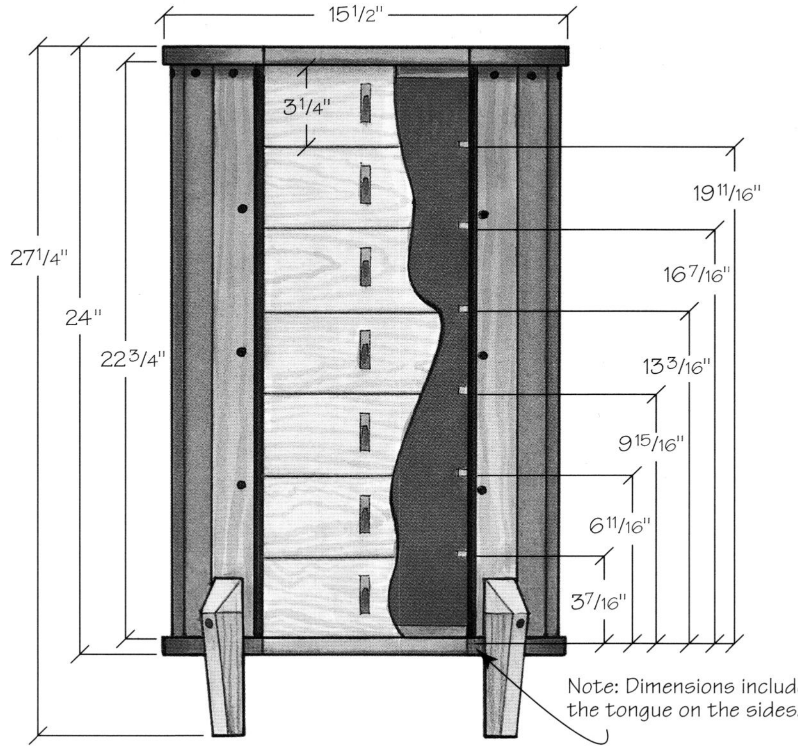

[1] GLUE THE EDGING TO THE INNER TOP AND BOTTOM
Cut the inner top, inner bottom and sides to the size given in the materials list. Cut the side thickeners off the ends of the pieces as you cut the inner top and bottom to their final lengths. Cut the two pieces of edging to size and glue them to the front edges of the top and bottom. Trim the edging flush with the surfaces of the top and bottom after the glue dries.

[2] DRAW THE CIRCLE
Draw a center line across both pieces. Measure in 5¾" (15cm) from the front edge and make a mark on the center line. Be very precise here—almost everything to come is based on this center mark. Use a compass to draw a 14" (35cm) diameter [7" (18cm)] radius) circle using that mark as the center. Double-check your work by measuring between the marks where the circle intersects with the front edge. They should be 8" (20cm) apart.

[3] STEP OFF THE DISTANCE AROUND THE CYLINDER
Draw perpendicular lines across the top, starting where the circle intersects the front edge. Draw a second set of lines ¾" (19mm) outside the first set. These pairs of lines indicate where the sides of the inner case go. Using a compass, step off the distance around the perimeter of the circle—make sure the pencil point is very sharp so it makes a precise mark. The steps should be about 2$^1/_{16}$" (5cm) wide; you may need to adjust the compass slightly. You want to start where the circle intersects the front edge on one side, and end exactly where it intersects the edge on the other. Note: There is no need to draw the layout on the bottom unless you need a fresh surface upon which to mark.

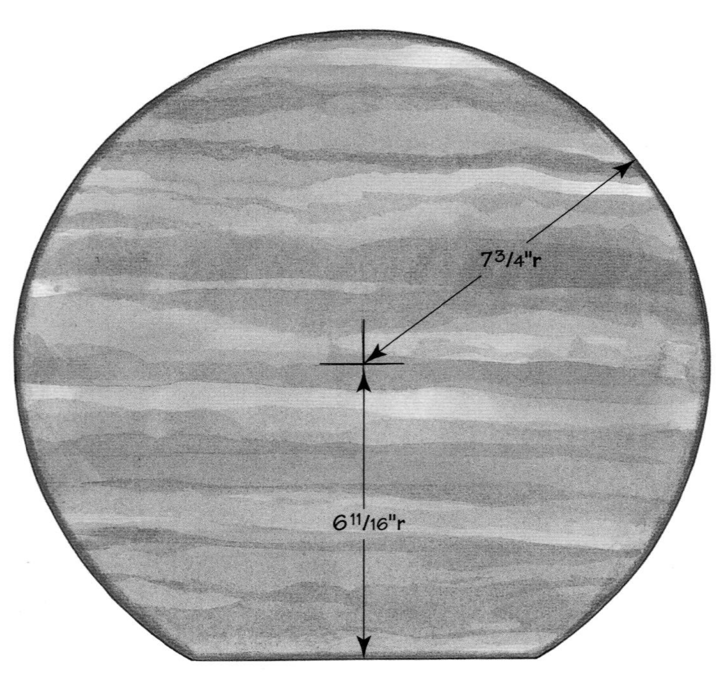

[4] MARK THE CENTERS OF THE STEPS

When the circle is stepped off precisely, connect the dots with straight lines. Then carefully mark the center of each of these lines.

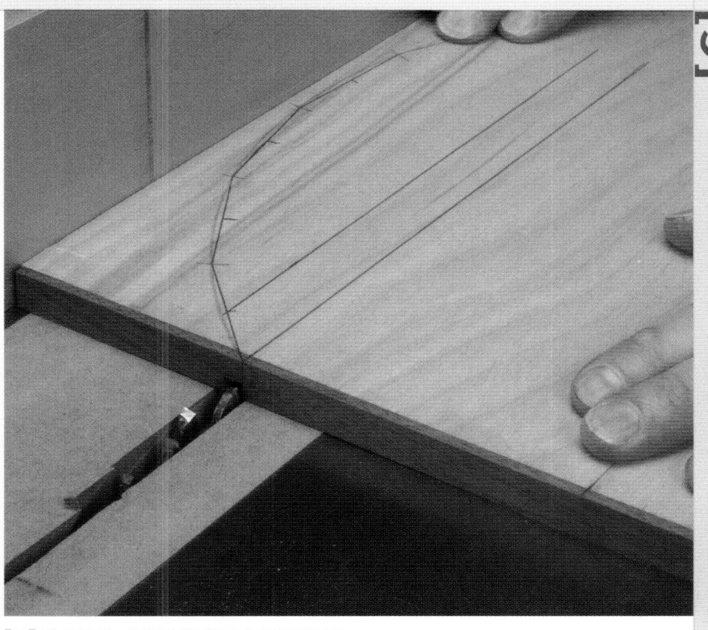

[5] DADO ACROSS THE TOP

To cut the grooves in the sides that will join them with the top and bottom, set up a 1/4"-wide (6mm) dado and adjust its height to 3/16" (5mm). Draw lines down the front edge of the top at the circle intersections. Adjust the rip fence, and cut a dado across the underside of the top just outside this line. Repeat the cut on the bottom, this time with the edging at the trailing end of the cut (to make a mirrored pair). Reset the saw to make a matching cut at the second line. Make the cuts in both pieces.

[6] CUT THE TONGUE ON THE SIDES

Increase the width of the dado blade to 5/8" (16mm) and lower its height to about 1/32" (less than 1mm). Adjust the rip fence so it is slightly more than 1/4" (6mm) from the blade. Cut tongues on the ends of the sides by running the pieces past the blade on edge. Cut the first tongue and check the fit by putting it into one of the grooves you just cut—the fit will probably be too tight. Bump the fence over and try again. Ideally the pieces should go together with firm hand pressure. Note: If you are nervous about cutting the pieces on edge, attach a tall auxiliary fence to the rip fence for added support.

[7] DADO THE PLYWOOD FOR DRAWER RUNNERS AND BEVEL THE FRONT EDGE OF THE SIDES

Set up a 1/4" (6mm) dado and adjust it to make a 1/8"-deep (3mm) cut. Cut dadoes across the sides for the drawer runners. (The spacing is shown in the front view on page 97). While the dado is set up, also cut 1/4"-deep (6mm) grooves for the back. Locate these grooves 1/4" (6mm) in from the back edges of the pieces.

[8] GLUE THE THICKENERS IN PLACE

Screw the inner top and bottom to the sides with the front edges of the sides flush with the front edges of the top and bottom (don't use glue—you'll need to disassemble them in a few minutes). Glue the side thickeners on either side of the side pieces—be careful not to get glue on the side pieces, but be sure the spacers butt up against the sides tightly. Cut the back thickeners to fit in between the side thickeners. Glue them in place as well, butting them up against the back edges of the sides.

[9] STACK THE TOP ON THE BOTTOM AND SCREW THE SPACERS TO THE THICKENERS

After the glue dries, disassemble the case. Cut two pieces of scrap 7/8" (2mm) wide and 10 1/2" (27cm) long. Screw these to the side thickeners on the bottom. Place the top on the bottom, using the scraps to keep everything aligned. Drive screws down through the top to fasten the pieces together. Keep the screws well inside the circular layout line. Drill a 3/8" (9mm) hole through both pieces, centering it on the original center mark you made on the top.

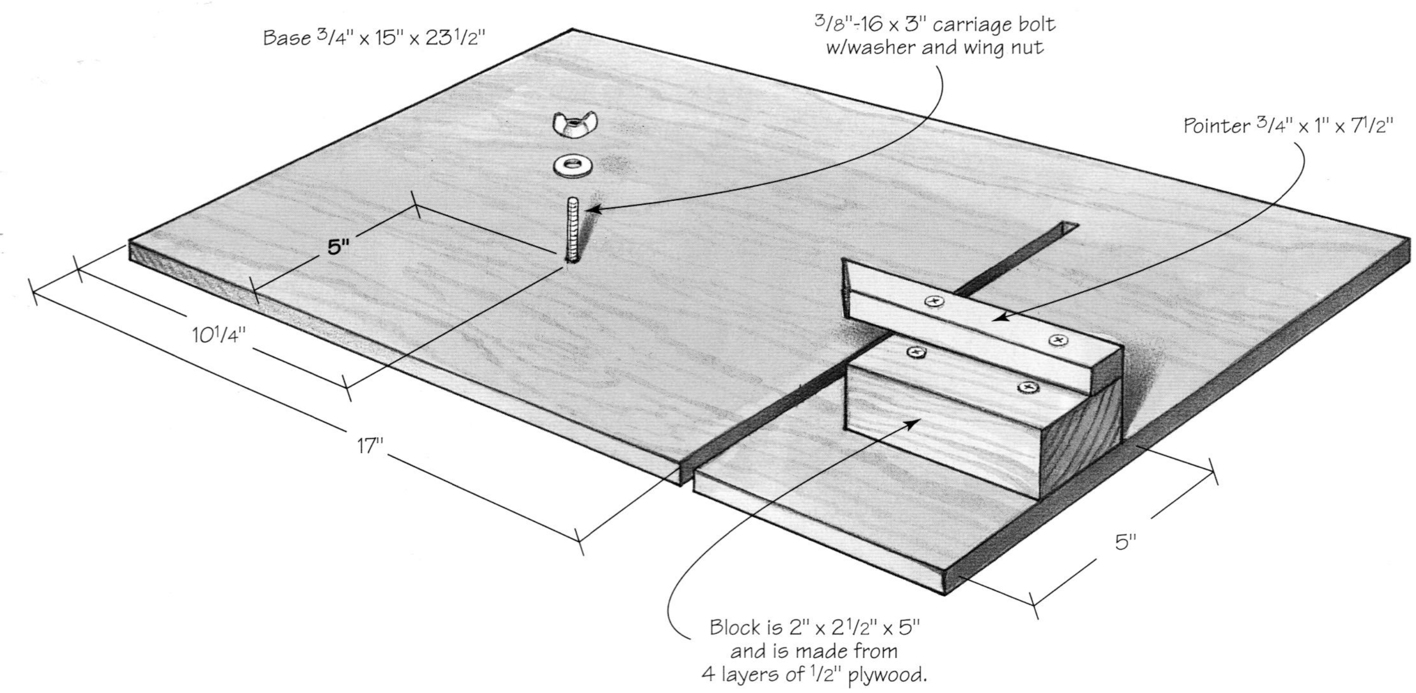

[10] CUT OFF THE CORNERS
After assembling the top and bottom sandwich, cut the corners off the sandwiched top and bottom. Guide the pieces through the cut with the miter gauge. Be sure to stay at least 1/4" (6mm) from the layout lines.

[11] CUT WITH THE FACETING SLED
Make up a sled to hold and position the pieces for faceting. Bolt the top/bottom sandwich in place. Rotate the pieces until the indicator arm aligns with the center mark on the first facet. Raise the blade high enough to cut through both pieces. Cut the first facet. Rotate the pieces so the arm aligns with the center of the second facet. Make the second cut. Continue in this manner until you have cut all the facets.

[12] BEVEL THE FRONT EDGE OF THE SIDES
Cut the drawer runners to size and glue them in their slots. Reassemble the inner case and mark the front edges of the sides to align with the facets cut on the top and bottom. Tilt the blade over to match this angle. Cut the sides so their front edges are flush with the facet. Note: You'll trim the corners of the drawer runners while making these cuts.

[13] CUT THE TRIM PIECE ON THE FRONT STAVES
Cut the staves and front trim pieces to size. Glue the front trim to the front staves. When the glue dries, scrape and sand the pieces to make their surfaces flush. Tilt the blade and cut the trim piece to the profile. Cut the other side of the front staves to an 98° bevel. Then bevel both edges of the regular staves at this same angle. The final width of the pieces is shown in the drawing, but double-check this against your top and bottom pieces.

[14] CUT SLOTS IN THE STAVES

Without changing the angle of the blade, adjust its height so it makes a $^1/_2$"-deep (13mm) cut. Run the staves along the fence to cut the slots for the splines.

[15] CHAMFER THE STAVES

Chamfer the outside corners of the staves with a V-cutter in a moulding head (alternately, you could tilt the blade to a 60° angle). For all pieces, make the cut on one side, then reset the fence and make the cut on the second sides. Also make a V-cut along the joint between the front staves and the front trim pieces.

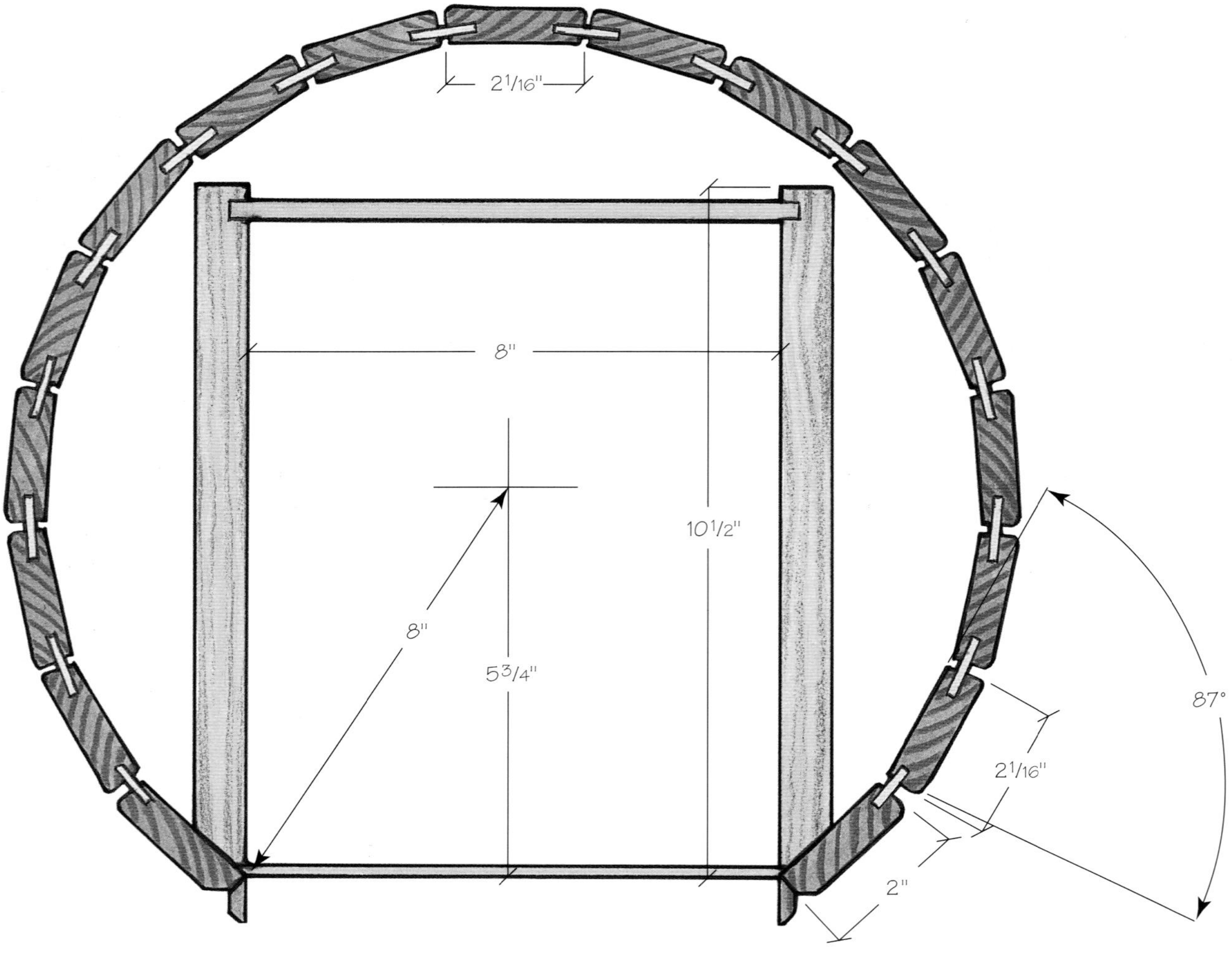

2$^1/_{16}$"
8"
10$^1/_2$"
8"
5$^3/_4$"
87°
2$^1/_{16}$"
2"

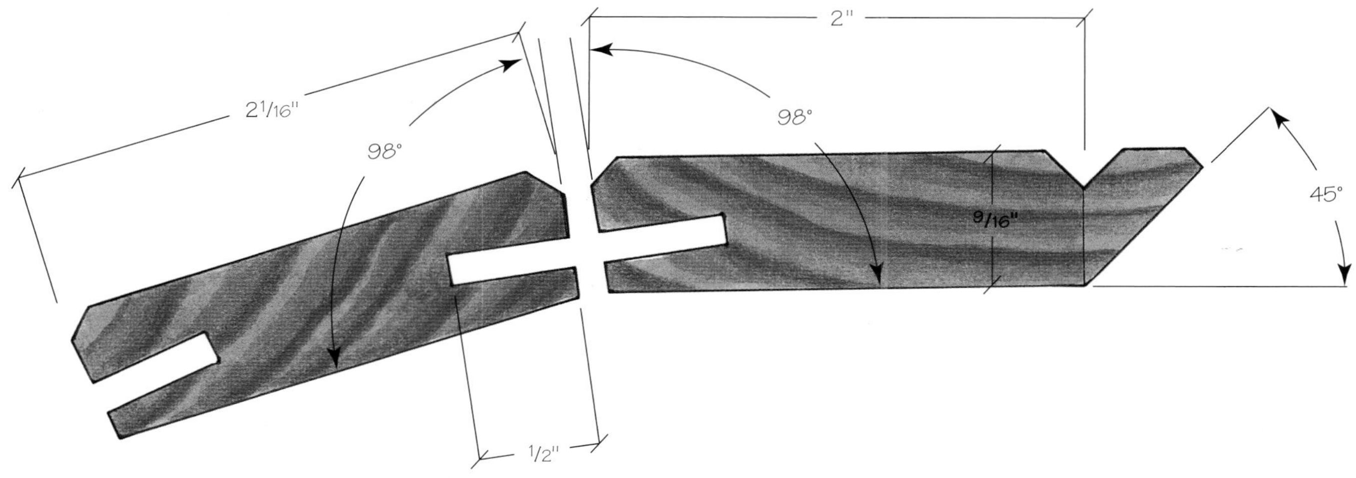

[16] DRILL THE STAVES FOR THE SCREW HOLES

Counterbore and drill the staves for the screws and plugs that will attach them. Make the 5/16" (8mm) counterbores first, then drill the screw holes. Center the holes from side to side and locate them 5/8" (16mm) in from the ends. Also counterbore and drill along the length of the front staves (as shown in the front view on page 97).

[17] CUT THE TOP AND BOTTOM ROUND

Glue the boards together to make up the top and bottom. Locate the center for each panel (as shown in the top view on page 97) and drill a 1/4"-diameter (6mm) hole that's 3/8" (9mm) deep. Be sure to drill the hole for the top in its underside. Make up a sled and adjust it to cut a 7³/4"-radius (20cm) circle. Place the top on the protruding bolt and push the sled past the blade, then pull it back. Turn the piece slightly and repeat. Continue cutting in this manner, slowly making the piece into a circle. Repeat with the bottom. If you have a 1/8" (3mm) roundover cutter for your moulding head, you can use the sled in tandem with the moulding head to round over the edges of both pieces. However, it is a lot easier to shape the pieces with a 1/8" (3mm) roundover bit in a router.

[18] CUT THE SLOTTED HOLES

The top and bottom are screwed to the inner top and bottom. Because you are attaching solid wood to plywood, you'll have to make slotted holes for the screws to allow for expansion and contraction. Cut the slotted holes in the inner top and in the solid wood bottom. Cut the counterbores first, with a 3/8" (9mm) straight bit in a router. Clamp a straightedge across the workpiece to serve as a guide. Before unclamping the straightedge, switch to a 3/16" (5mm) straight bit to make the actual slot.

[19] ATTACH THE FRONT STAVES

Attach the inner top and inner bottom to the sides with glue and screws. Cut the back to size and slide it into its grooves before going any further. Turn the assembly upside down and screw it to the underside of the top. Leave it upside down as you attach the staves. Start by screwing the front staves in place. They should end up flush with the sides' inner faces.

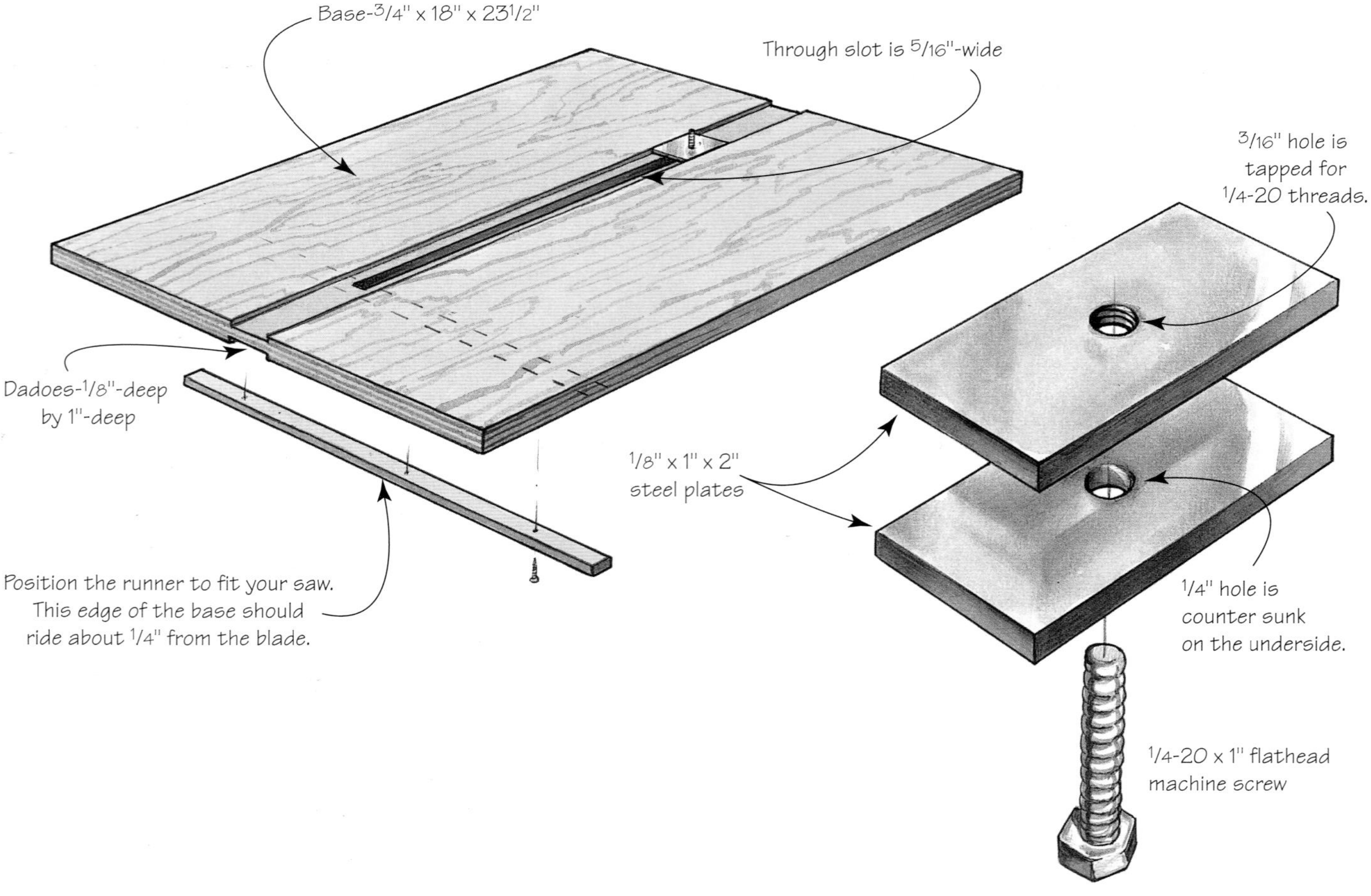

Base-3/4" x 18" x 23 1/2"

Through slot is 5/16"-wide

3/16" hole is tapped for 1/4-20 threads.

Dadoes-1/8"-deep by 1"-deep

1/8" x 1" x 2" steel plates

Position the runner to fit your saw. This edge of the base should ride about 1/4" from the blade.

1/4" hole is counter sunk on the underside.

1/4-20 x 1" flathead machine screw

[20] ADD A REGULAR STAVE

Once the front staves are in place, add the regular staves. Stain or dye the splines an eye-catching color, and glue one in the forward side of each stave. (The middle stave in the back gets two splines, one in either side. But don't glue these yet—you might need to adjust the width of this piece to make everything fit.) Screw the staves to the inner top and bottom, leaving a slight gap [about 1/16" (1mm)] between the pieces as you go. Work both sides from front to back. If necessary, you can trim the last stave to fit.

[21] TRIM THE STAVES

Plane the bottoms of the staves flush with the inner bottom. Screw the bottom in place.

[22] INSTALL A FOOT

Cut the feet to shape (see "Making the Feet" on page 110). Notch the bottom for each foot where it protrudes past the staves. Instead of using the table saw to do this, simply make cuts at either side with a handsaw, then clean out in between with a chisel. Glue and screw the legs to the cylinder.

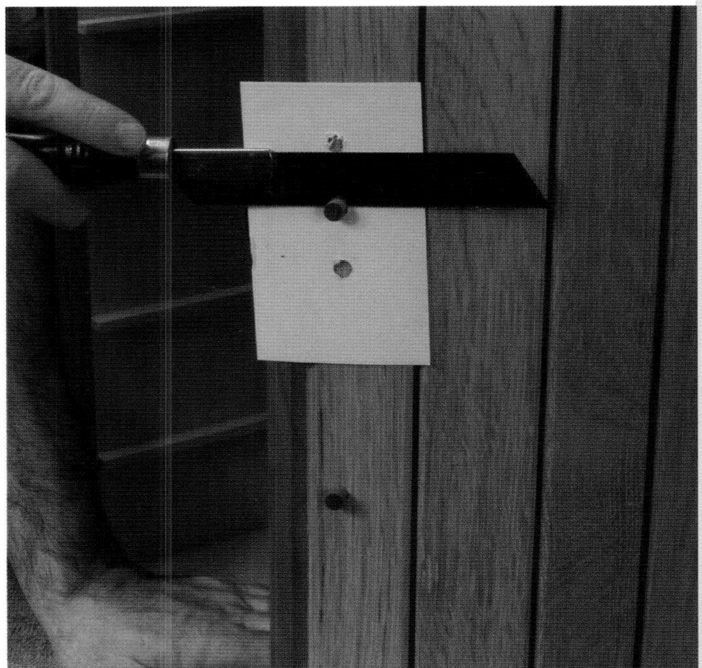

[23] SAW OFF A PLUG

Cut plugs for the screw holes with a plug cutter. Apply glue to the plugs and glue them in place. Once the glue dries, cut the plugs off with a flush-cut saw, and sand away the saw marks. Note: I use a 3" × 5" (8cm × 13cm) card as a shield to help protect the surface surrounding each plug.

[24] RESAW THE DRAWER FRONTS

Cut the stock for the drawers to size, leaving the drawer front about 1⁄8" (3mm) oversize for now. Resaw the drawer fronts, cutting the inner "halves" that will receive the joinery 3⁄8" (9mm) thick. Then cut these inner halves to size, leaving the mating pieces oversized. Mark the pairs so you can reunite them later.

[25] CUT FINGER JOINTS IN A DRAWER PIECE

On all but the top drawer front, start cutting the finger joints with the top edge of the drawer fronts and backs (including the top drawer back) against the key in the jig. Cut the matching part of the joint on the side pieces.

[26] CUT FINGER JOINTS ON THE TOP FRONT

For the top drawer front, remove the key from the jig and clamp a stop block 3⁄4" (19mm) from the blade. Make the first cut on either end with the top edge butted against the stop. Then remove the stop block and replace the key. Continue cutting the joint as usual.

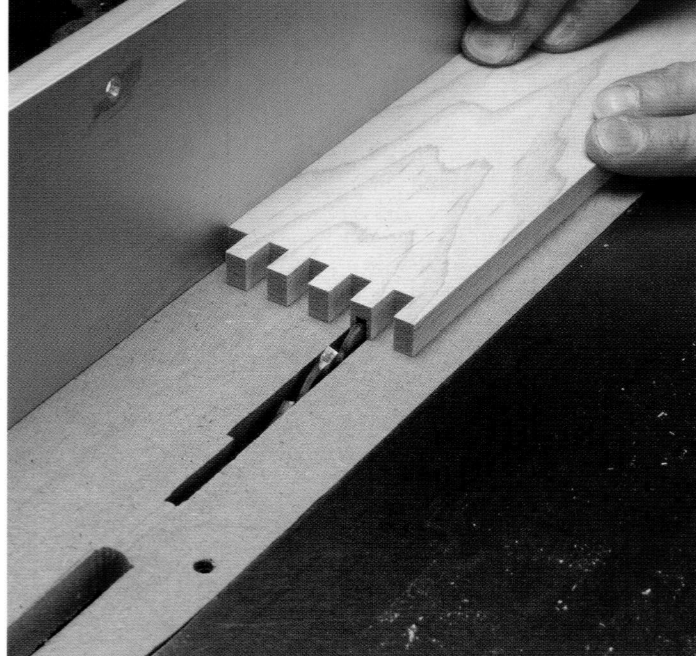

[27] CUT THE SLOTS FOR THE BOTTOM

Cut the slots for the bottom so they run out through one of the fingers on the drawer sides. This way, the hole created will be hidden when you glue on the drawer face. You'll be able to see the hole at the back of the drawer, but only if you pull it out all the way.

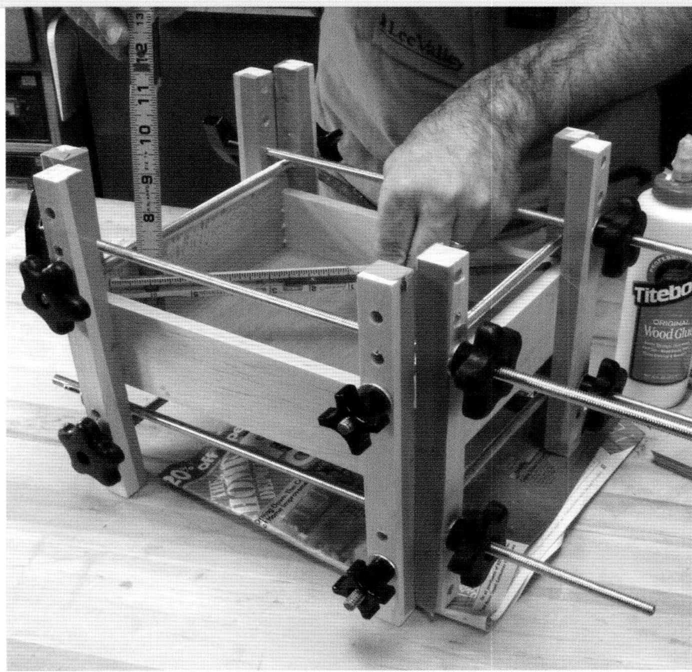

[28] GLUE UP A DRAWER

Cut the drawer bottoms to size. Sand the inside of the drawers and glue them together. You'll find this process a lot easier if you make up a set of box clamps. Remember to insert the bottom into its grooves before clamping the parts together. Check the diagonal measurements (they should be equal) to make sure the drawer is square.

[29] SAND THE DRAWER FACE

Carefully sand the drawer fronts flush with the ends of the fingers. Note: I find it easiest to keep the drawer faces flat if I tape a sheet of sandpaper to the saw table and work the face down by scrubbing the whole drawer across the abrasive surface.

Face Gluing

When making a project that involves wide glued-up panels, find a commercial shop that will run your pieces through their wide belt (or drum) sander. These machines make short work of flattening glue lines and getting the pieces to a uniform thickness and flatness. It is well worth the money you'll spend to have the pieces sanded for you.

[30] SCREW A PULL TO THE DRAWER

Glue the drawer faces to the fronts of the drawers. When the glue dries, plane or scrape the overhanging edges of the face flush with the rest of the front. Drill the drawers for the pulls, countersinking the hole on the inside of each drawer. Fit the drawers to the case, sanding and scraping as necessary to get a good fit. Apply finish—several coats of wiping varnish, for example. Once everything is dry, screw the pulls (see "Making the Pulls" on page 112) to the drawers. Apply a little paraffin to the sides of the drawers and their runners for smooth action.

Making the Feet

As simple as they appear, the feet require a series of eight separate operations to complete. None of the steps is particularly difficult—the key is to do them in the right order so you don't cut away any of the surfaces you need before you use them. Cut the pieces to the sizes given in the materials list, then follow these how-to instructions.

[1] TAPER THE FRONT

Lay out the front taper (as shown in the side view on page 97). Align the leg on a piece of scrap plywood with the layout line aligned with the edge of the plywood. Screw a fence to the plywood along the leg's back edge and add a stop behind the piece to help hold it in position. Cut the front tapers on all the legs.

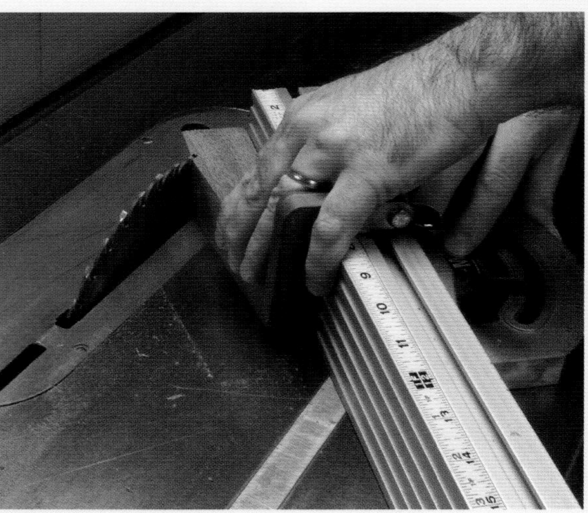

[2] BEVEL THE TOP

Adjust the miter gauge to cut a 41° angle and cut the bevel on the tops of the legs. Note: Leave a $^{5}/_{16}$"-wide (8mm) flat on the top of each leg.

[3] CUT THE BEVELS ON THE FRONT OF A FOOT

Tilt the blade to a 63° angle and bevel the front sides of each leg. Run the pieces through the cut twice with the tapered face down on the saw table. The flat left between the two pieces should be $^{1}/_{2}$"-wide (13mm) or slightly wider. Note: With a right-hand tilt saw, you'll need to position the fence to the left of the blade.

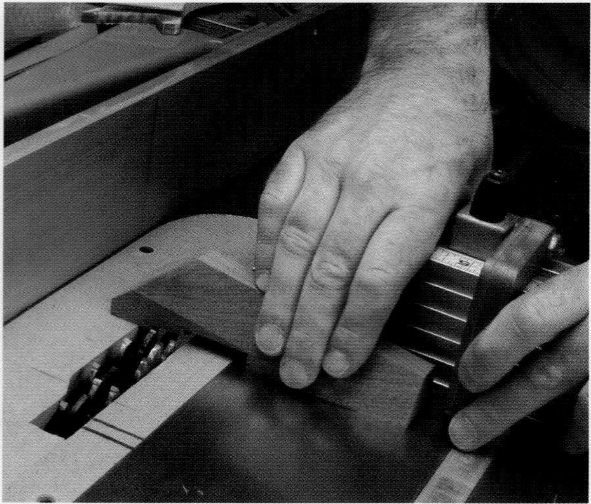

[4] DADO THE FOOT

Set up a $^{3}/_{4}$"-wide (19mm) dado blade (the exact width is not important) and notch each foot as shown. Leave about $^{1}/_{2}$" (13mm) of material at the top end of the notch to support the piece during subsequent cuts.

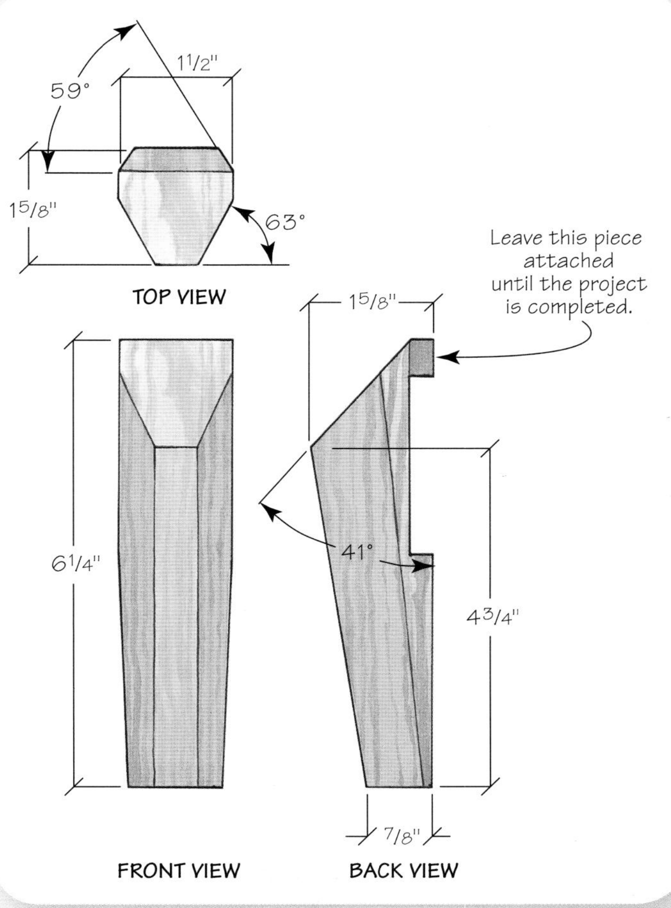

[5] BEVEL THE BACK EDGES

Change back to a regular blade and tilt it over to a 59° angle. To bevel the back edges of each foot, start by cutting each piece from top to bottom. At first, cut the pieces a little wide, then bump the fence over until the bevel just kisses the inside corner of the notch. For the second side, cut the pieces from bottom to top. The lower part of the leg won't touch the fence, but the upper part should provide a straight reference surface. Keep this part against the fence as you cut.

[6] SAND THE FEET

Swap your saw blade for a sanding disk and tilt the disk 61° to match the bevel on the front of the legs. Carefully sand the front bevels to remove the small triangle left between the front and back bevels. You can also do this with a stationary belt sander, but as this is a table saw book...

[7] DRILL THE PIECES FOR SCREWS

Drill and counterbore the legs for screws and plugs. Then cut away the excess material you left at the top of the notch with a handsaw and a sharp chisel.

Making the Pulls

One of the most challenging parts of designing a piece of furniture is drawer and/or door pull selection. Sometimes you can find just the right pull in a catalog. With an original design, however, you often have to design the pulls along with the rest of the piece or it simply won't look right. It took several tries to come up with the pulls for this project.

What follows is the cutting sequence for making these pulls. Keep in mind that these pieces are quite small—too small to hold safely with your fingers when you're cutting them. You must devise strategies for holding the pieces securely while keeping them registered for accuracy. I screw the pieces to a carrier board. I drill for the screws near the beginning of the process, locating the holes where I ultimately want them for attaching to the drawers.

[1] DRILL THE BIG CURVES
Start with a piece of stock that is 1/2" × 1/2" × 18" (13mm × 13mm × 457mm). This should give you enough material for nine pulls. Drill a series of 1"-diameter (25mm) holes along the length of the piece, starting the first hole 1 1/2" (39mm) in from one end. Space the holes 1 7/8" (36mm) on center. Use a piece of scrap as a fence. When you make the first hole, you'll also drill into the fence. The partial hole created in the fence will help support the bit and keep it from wandering on the subsequent holes.

[2] DRILL THE SCREW HOLES
Carefully measure 3/8" (9mm) from the edge of each partial hole and draw a square line across the stock. Set up a fence on the drill press and drill a 3/32" (less than 1mm) hole on each of the lines. Be sure to position the fence so that the holes are centered across the width of the piece. Make the holes 3/8" (9mm) deep.

[3] DRILL THE MOUNTING HOLES
Cut a scrap to 3/4" × 2 1/2" × 17" (19mm × 63mm × 432mm) to serve as a carrier board. Drill a series of nine 1/8" (3mm) holes through the scrap. Use a fence to make sure the holes are centered along a line 1" in from the edge. The holes should be spaced 1 3/4" (44mm) on center and the first hole should be 3/4" (19mm) in from one end. Counterbore the holes so a 5/8" (8mm) screw protrudes about 5/16" (8mm).

[TIP] ***Cutting pieces that are screwed to a carrier board is a very safe way of dealing with small parts. But you have to remember that there is a screw buried in the piece. Locate that screw BEFORE you cut. You absolutely don't want the blade to hit the screw.***

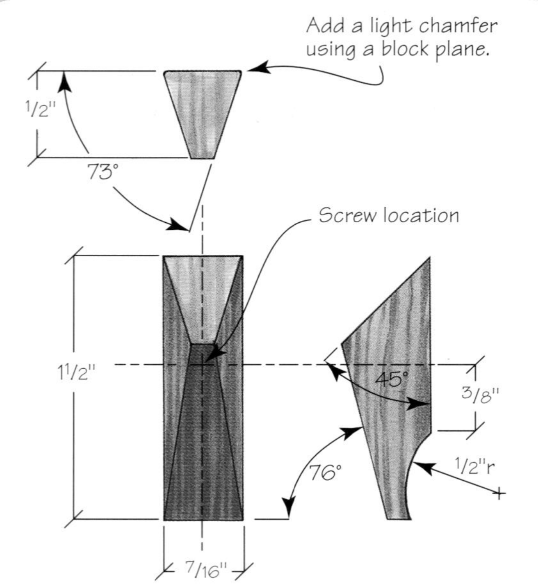

[4] CUT THE PULLS TO LENGTH

Cut the blanks roughly to length, sawing them apart at the end of the curve opposite the screw hole. Use 5⁄8" (16mm) screws to fasten the blanks to the carrier with their curved ends overhanging the edge. Use a square to make sure the pieces are perpendicular to the edge, and tighten the screws. Set the fence so the saw cuts along the edge of the carrier. Feed the carrier through the cut.

[5] TAPER THE PULLS

Tilt the blade on your saw to 76°. Turn the carrier board on edge and adjust the fence so the pulls will be 1⁄8" (3mm) thick where they touch the saw table. Run the carrier along the fence to make the cut.

[6] CUT THE OPPOSITE END

Loosen the screws and turn the pieces 180° so their opposite ends are pointed down. Tilt the blade to a 45° angle. Adjust the fence so the blade cuts 7⁄16" (11mm) up the face of the carrier board. Feed the carrier through the cut.

[7] CUT THE SIDE ANGLES

Turn the pieces so they are parallel to the long edge of the carrier board. Tilt the blade to a 76° angle. Adjust the fence so it cuts through the carrier and just kisses the corner of the pulls. Cut the first three pulls, then carefully back the carrier out of the cut. Turn these three pulls around and cut the second side. Remove the cut pulls and move the next three up on the board. Cut them, then move up the last group. Cutting this way keeps the carrier intact.

TRIANGLE CHEST [10]

If you're looking to break away from the ordinary, this is a great place to start. In both form and materials, this playful little stand is a pretty big departure from traditional woodworking. All the while, however, it plays to the table saw's strengths: straight lines, tapers and joinery that can be cut with a dado blade.

The design grew out of my fascination with the triangle as a structural element. In both architecture and structural engineering, triangles play an integral part—think roof trusses and steel frame bridges. They're inherently strong and have a geometric precision and logic to them. Why, then, don't triangles show up more often in furniture? Perhaps it's because squares and rectangles are far easier to build. And practicality is probably a factor, too—triangular spaces don't hold as much stuff. Regardless, the triangle is a fun shape to incorporate into a piece of furniture.

As for the materials used here, the case and the drawers are made from Baltic birch plywood, its edges left unapologetically exposed. The legs are simply dowels colored with metallic spray paint. I stained the case with Woodburst Color wood stain, then finished with several coats of lacquer.

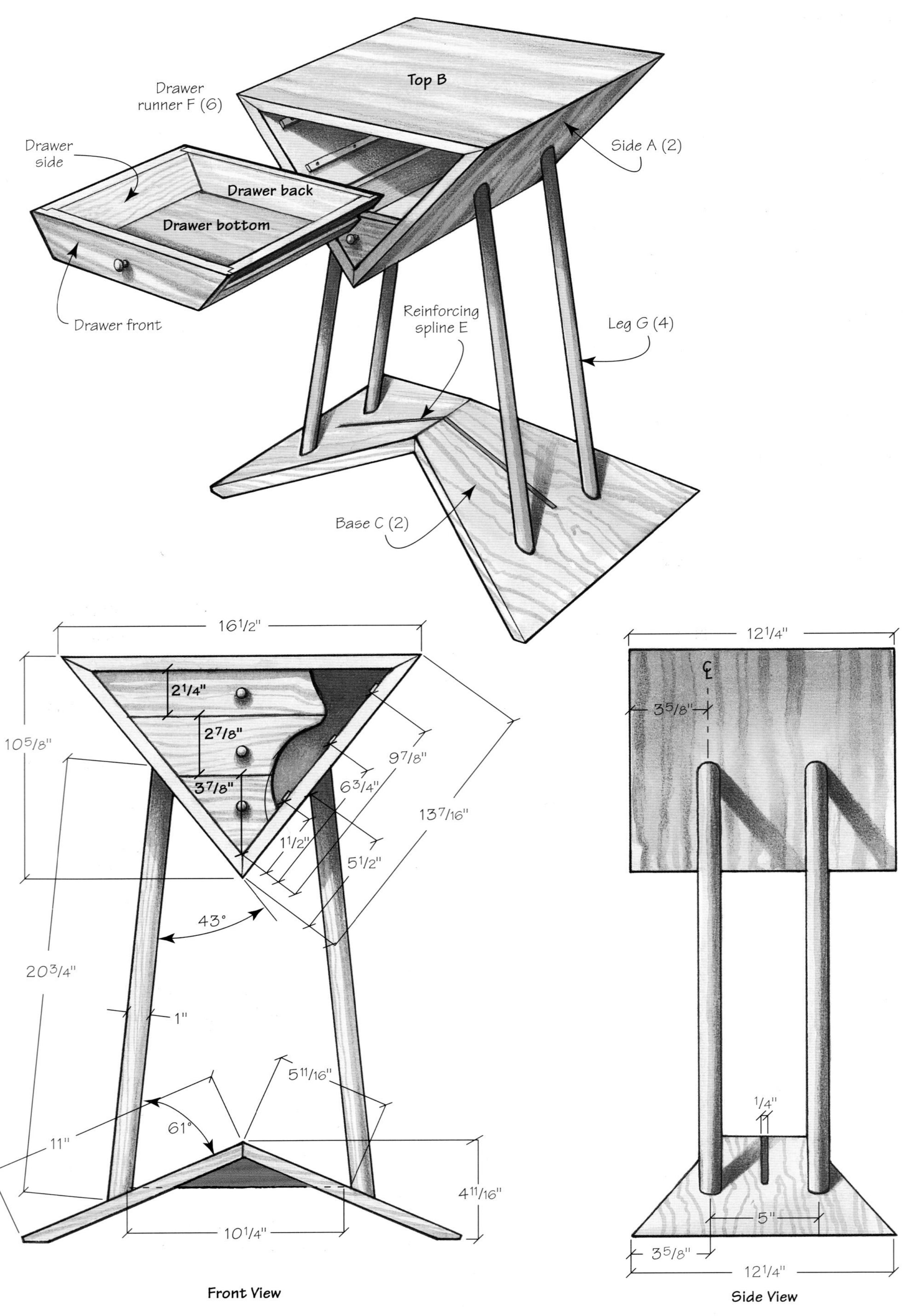
Top B
Drawer runner F (6)
Drawer side
Drawer back
Drawer bottom
Side A (2)
Drawer front
Reinforcing spline E
Leg G (4)
Base C (2)
16 1/2"
10 5/8"
2 1/4"
2 7/8"
3 7/8"
9 7/8"
6 3/4"
13 7/16"
1 1/2"
5 1/2"
43°
20 3/4"
1"
5 11/16"
61°
11"
4 11/16"
10 1/4"
12 1/4"
3 5/8"
1/4"
5"
3 5/8"
12 1/4"
Front View

Side View

[CASE] inches (millimeters)

REFERENCE	QUANTITY	PART	STOCK	THICKNESS	(mm)	WIDTH	(mm)	LENGTH	(mm)	COMMENTS
A	2	sides	plywood	5/8	(16)	12 1/4	(311)	13 7/16	(341)	Cut 1/4" (6mm) too long
B	1	top	plywood	5/8	(16)	12 1/4	(311)	16 1/2	(419)	Cut 1/4" (6mm) too long
C	2	base	plywood	5/8	(16)	12 1/4	(311)	11	(279)	Cut 1/4" (6mm) too long
D	1	back	plywood	1/4	(6)	9 1/2	(241)	14 1/2	(368)	
E	1	reinforcing spline	hardwood	1/4	(6)	9 1/2	(241)	14 1/2	(368)	
F	6	drawer runners	hardwood	1/8	(3)	1/2	(13)	11 1/4	(286)	
G	4	legs	hardwood	1	(25)	20 3/4	(527)			Cut 1" (25mm) too long
[TOP DRAWER]										
H	1	face	hardwood	3/8	(9)	2 1/4	(57)	14 1/8	(359)	
I	2	front/back	hardwood	3/8	(9)	2 1/16	(52)	13 3/16	(335)	
J	2	sides	hardwood	3/8	(9)	2 5/8	(67)	10 5/8	(270)	
K	1	bottom	plywood	1/8	(3)	9 3/4	(246)	10 5/8	(270)	
[MIDDLE DRAWER]										
L	1	face	hardwood	3/8	(9)	2 7/8	(73)	10 5/8	(270)	
M	2	front/back	hardwood	3/8	(9)	2 9/16	(65)	9 13/16	(249)	
N	2	sides	hardwood	3/8	(9)	3 1/4	(82)	10 5/8	(270)	
O	1	bottom	plywood	1/8	(3)	9 3/4	(246)	6 7/16	(163)	
[BOTTOM DRAWER]										
P	1	face	hardwood	3/8	(9)	3 7/8	(98)	6	(152)	
Q	2	front/back	hardwood	3/8	(9)	2	(51)	5 1/8	(130)	
R	2	sides	hardwood	3/8	(9)	2 1/2	(63)	10 5/8	(270)	
S	1	bottom	plywood	1/8	(3)	9 3/4	(246)	3 11/16	(94)	

[HARDWARE]

8	#8 × 1 1/4" Screws
24	#6 × 3/4" Screws
24	#4 × 1/2" Screws
3	5/8" Diameter Brass Knobs

[1] MAKE A FULL SIZE DRAWING

Make a full-size drawing of the front view. Start the drawing with a vertical center line and try to make the layout as accurately and symmetrically as possible—you'll be using this drawing to check your miter angles.

[2] CUT PIECES TO SIZE

Cut the plywood for the case sides, top and base to the sizes indicated in the materials list. Be sure to cut all the pieces about 1/4" (6mm) longer than the finished size. This will give you a little wiggle room when it comes to cutting the miters. Also cut three test pieces for fine-tuning the miter cuts. These pieces should be the same lengths as the sides and top, but they only have to be about 5" or 6" (160mm) wide.

[3] SCREW AN AUXILIARY FENCE TO THE REGULAR FENCE

Because the case sides come together to form acute angles, you have to the miters by running the pieces past the blade vertically. (The blade won't tilt far enough to cut the pieces flat on the table.) Attach an auxiliary fence to the face of your saw fence. Make it about 6" (160mm) tall, (the exact height doesn't matter). What is important is that the top edge of the fence ends up parallel to the saw table. To make sure, rest the bottom edge of the auxiliary fence on the table when you attach it to the saw fence.

[4] SET THE MITER ANGLE WITH A T-BEVEL

Cut the miter at the bottom of the case first. Measure the angle on your drawing with a protractor, then transfer it to a T-bevel and use the T-bevel to set the blade angle. The angle should be about 38°. Note—Be sure to hold the T-bevel perpendicular to the table or the angle won't be true. Also note that if your saw tilts to the right, you'll need to shift the fence to the left side of the blade.

[5] MEASURE FROM THE CUT TO THE TOP OF THE FENCE

Once the blade angle is set, lower the blade and bump the fence over so the blade will cut through the auxiliary fence. Turn on the saw and raise the blade, cutting through the face of the auxiliary fence. Note: Don't move the fence over so far that the blade cuts through the face of the saw's stock fence. Stop the saw, lower the blade and measure from the top of the saw-kerf to the top of the auxiliary fence. Make a note of this measurement; you'll need it several times.

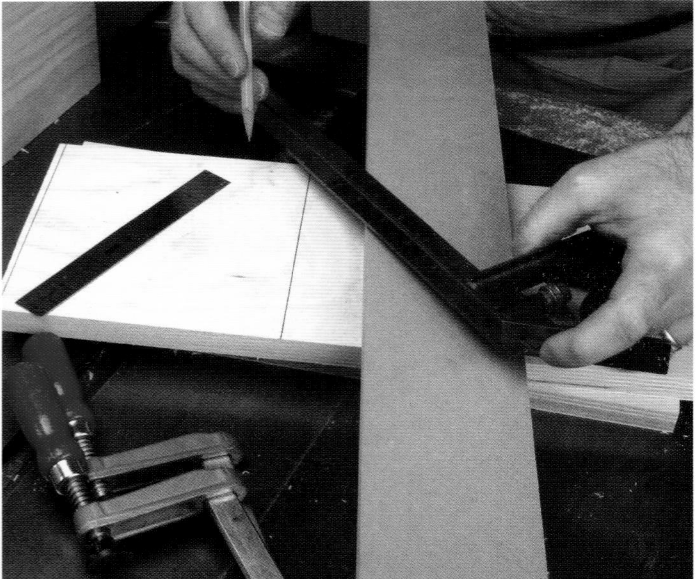

[6] CLAMP THE GUIDE BOARD TO A TEST PIECE

On one of your test pieces, draw a line 1/8" (3mm) in from one end and square to the edge. This line represents the tip of the miter cut. Draw a second line across the piece, offsetting it the distance you measured in step five. Clamp a guide board [3" (80mm) wide × 20" (521mm) long] along this second line. Use a square to make sure the guide board is perpendicular to the edge of the test piece.

[7] MAKE A MITER CUT

Cut the miter by running the guide board along the top of the auxiliary fence. Be sure to keep the workpiece flat against the face of the fence. Mark and cut the second test piece to match. Hold the pieces together and check them against your drawing. If necessary, tweak the blade angle (more upright to close the angle, more angled to open it) and recut the test pieces. Note: When adjusting the blade angle, lower the blade beneath the table so it doesn't bind against the auxiliary fence. Then raise it again to make the cut. When you are satisfied with the miter angle, make the miter cut on the bottom ends of the side pieces, laying out the cuts and attaching the guide board as you did with the test pieces. Save the cutoffs to use as clamping blocks.

[8] MARK THE LENGTH OF THE TOP

Repeat the process to cut the miters that join the sides to the top. Note that the angle is shallower (about 26°), so the blade will exit the auxiliary fence in a slightly different position. You'll need to remeasure to establish your new blade-to-fence-top measurement. Miter the square end of one of the side test pieces and one end of the top test piece. Tweak the blade angle and recut as necessary until the pieces come together and match the angle on your drawing. Cut the angles on the side pieces—cut them to length in the process. Hold the side pieces together and use them to mark the top piece for length. Miter both ends of the top.

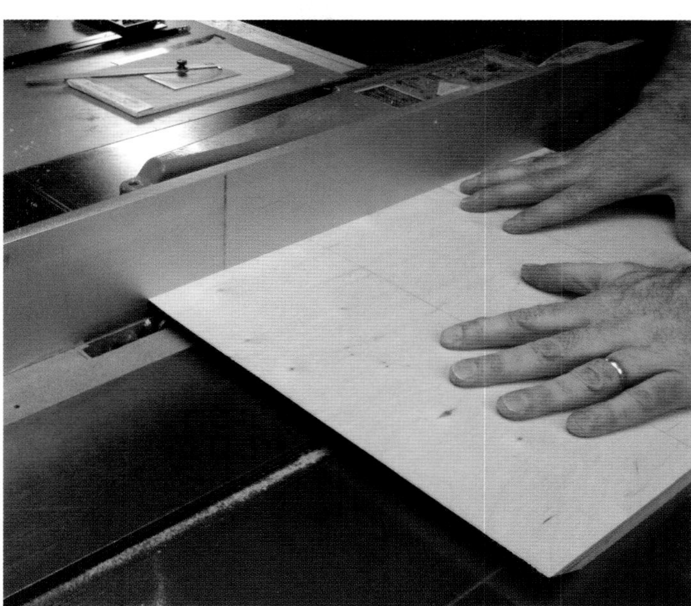

[9] CUT THE GROOVE FOR THE BACK IN THE TOP

Set up a 1⁄4" (3mm) dado blade and cut a groove for the back panel in the three case pieces. Locate each groove 3⁄8" (9mm) in from the back edge of the piece.

[10] GLUE THE GLUE BLOCKS IN PLACE

To prepare to glue the case together, you need to attach glue blocks at the ends of the pieces so you have a way to apply pressure directly across the joints. Fasten the clamping blocks to the pieces with a combination of double-faced tape and glue.

[11] DRILL FOR THE LEGS

Before gluing the case together, drill two $3/16$" (5mm) diameter holes in each side for attaching the legs. Countersink the holes on the inside faces of the sides.

[12] INSTALL THE RUNNERS

Before gluing, you will also add the drawer runners to the sides. Cut the runners to size. Clamp the two sides together along the bottom miter. Cut a scrap of $1/4$" (6mm) plywood to serve as a spacer. Starting with the top runners, cut the spacer to the width shown in the front view. Hold the spacer in the V that the sides form to keep the runner in the right position as you glue and screw it in place. Cut the spacer down to do the middle and bottom runners.

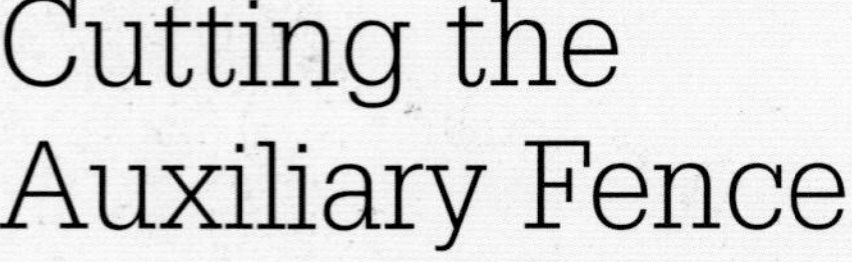

Cutting the Auxiliary Fence

When I cut miters with the help of an auxiliary fence, I often set up the saw so the blade actually cuts through the auxiliary fence's face. There are two benefits: First, the fence functions as a vertical, zero-clearance throat insert that helps prevent tear-out. Second, cutting through the fence means the cut actually occurs above the surface of the table, which keeps your workpiece from riding on the fragile point of a freshly cut miter.

[13] CLAMP THE CASE

Cut the back to size, then sand and prefinish it. Apply glue to the mitered surfaces and clamp the case together. Be sure to put the back in place before the glue dries.

[14] MITER THE BASE
Cut the pieces for the base to size. Tilt the blade to a 64° angle and cut one end of each piece to create the miter where the pieces come together. To cut the angle on the opposite ends of the pieces, leave the blade at the same angle but run the pieces on end against the fence as you did for the case miters. (No need for an auxiliary fence this time.)

[15] TAPER THE BASE
Lay out the tapers on the face of one of the base pieces. Place the piece on a carrier board with one of the layout lines aligned with the edge of the carrier. Attach fences to the carrier board to hold the piece in this position. Adjust the fence so the blade cuts along the side of the carrier board. Cut one side of each base piece. Reset the fences and cut the tapers on the second side.

Gluing Miters

Gluing miter joints is tricky because there typically isn't a good way to apply clamping pressure directly across the joint. To solve this problem, I attach clamping blocks (often the offcut from cutting the miter) to the workpieces. For a time I used double-sided tape to do the job, but found it often slipped under pressure. Then I tried gluing the blocks in place. This works, but can be difficult to clean up. Lately I've used a combination of the two methods. I dab a little glue on the blocks at either end and in the middle, then fill in between with double-sided tape. This way, the blocks stay in place but aren't a nuisance to remove.

[16] DRILL THE BASE
Lay out and drill $^3/_{16}$" (5mm) holes in the base pieces for attaching the legs. Countersink the holes on the underside of the pieces. Attach clamping blocks and glue up the base as you did with the case.

[17] CUT THE SLOT IN THE BASE

Make up a sled to carry the base across the saw in an upside down position. Set up a 1/4" (6mm) dado and adjust it to make as deep a cut as possible. Position the rip fence to center the cut across the width of the base. Screw the base to the sled through the holes you drilled for the legs. Guide it along the fence to make the cut. Cut the reinforcing spline to fit the slot.

[18] CUT THE REINFORCING SPLINE

Slip the reinforcing spline into its slot in the base. Trace the angles onto both of its faces. Align the spline on a carrier board as you did when tapering the base pieces. Set the rip fence so the blade cuts a heavy 1/16" (1mm) away from the edge of the carrier board. This will leave extra material so the edge of the spline won't be quite flush with the surfaces of the base—it's easier to deal with this way. Make the cut, then flip the piece end for end and make the second cut.

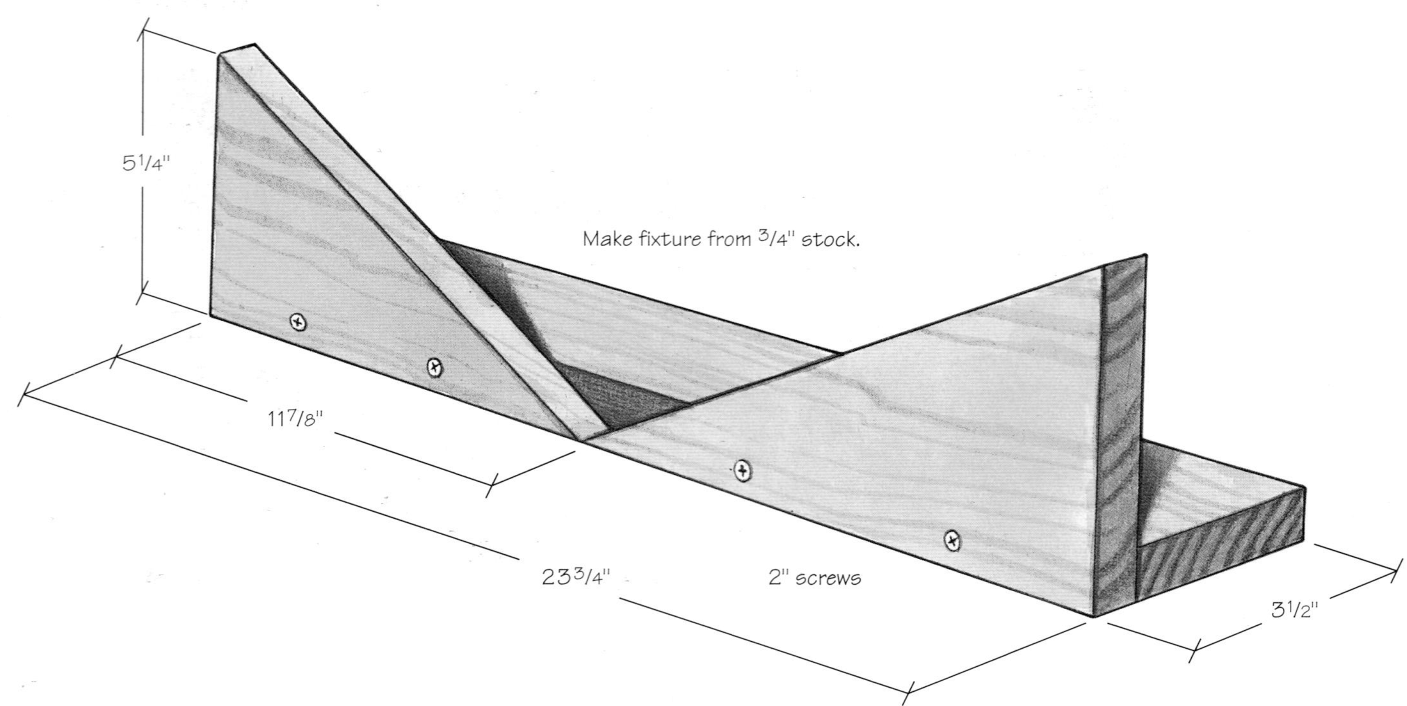

[19] CUT THE FIRST MITER ON A LEG

Cut the dowels for the legs roughly to length, leaving yourself about 1" (25mm) extra on each piece. Cut the angle on the top end of each piece, guiding the pieces through the cut with the miter gauge. The angle should be about 43°, but check it against your drawing.

[20] DRAW A LINE ACROSS THE LEG

One of the tricky parts of working with cylinders is getting the various cuts oriented properly. With these legs, the miter cuts need to be parallel to each other. To make this happen, you have to be sure the leg doesn't rotate in between cuts—this is much easier to say than do. Start with a piece of $^1/_2$"-thick (13mm) material—a piece of $^1/_2$" (13mm) MDF is ideal. Butt the mitered end up against its edge and draw a horizontal center line. On this line, drill a pilot hole for a screw $^3/_{16}$" (5mm) in from the low side of the cut. Screw a short length of scrap [$^1/_2$" × 1" × 3" (13mm × 25mm × 76mm)] to the leg to keep it from turning.

[21] CUT THE SECOND MITER

Reset the miter gauge to cut the bottom miter on each leg. The angle should be about 61°, but check your drawing. Mark the first leg for length. Add a spacer along the miter gauge fence to allow clearance for the block on the end of the leg. Position a stop to control the length of the legs. Cut the first leg and double-check it against the drawing.

[22] CUT A GROOVE FOR THE DRAWER RUNNER

Cut the drawer parts to size. Cut grooves in the sides for the drawer runners. Check the fit of the pieces in the case. They should slide on the runners without binding or rattling.

[23] DADO THE DRAWER SIDES

Cut 1/8"-deep (3mm) dadoes across the drawer sides to receive the fronts and backs. Make the dadoes for the fronts 1/8" (3mm) wide (cut with a regular saw blade) and those for the backs, 3/8" (9mm) wide (cut with a dado head).

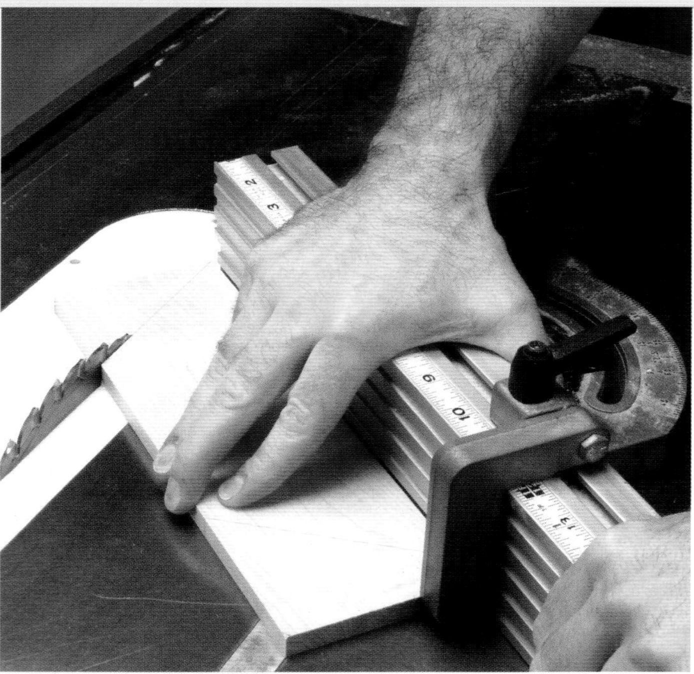

[24] CUT THE DRAWER FRONT TO LENGTH (AT AN ANGLE)

For each drawer, place the drawer sides on their runners and measure in between to check the length of the front and back. Be sure to compensate for the angle. Cut the fronts and backs to the proper length and angle with the help of the miter gauge.

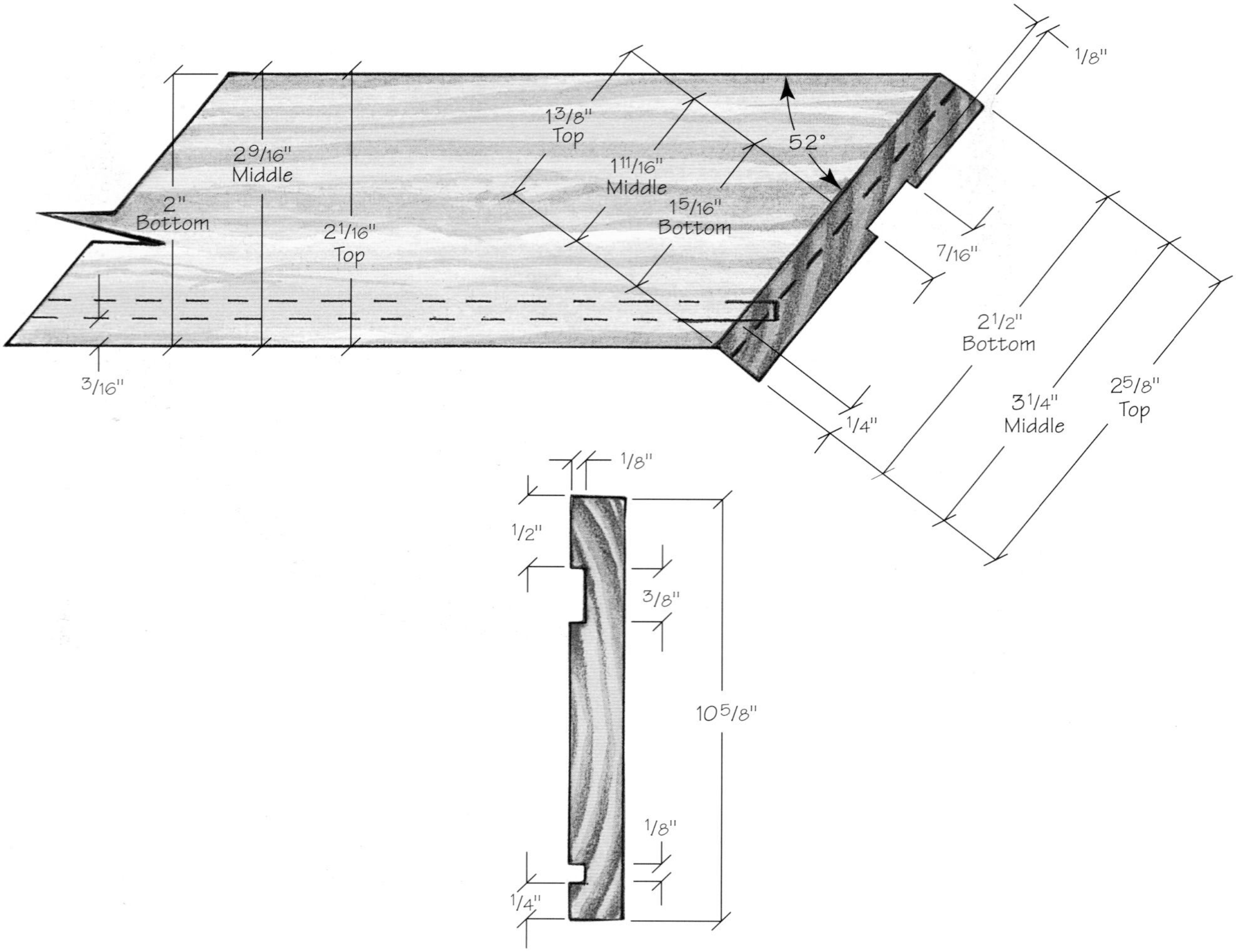

2" Bottom
2 9/16" Middle
2 1/16" Top
3/16"
1 3/8" Top
1 11/16" Middle
1 5/16" Bottom
52°
1/8"
7/16"
1/4"
2 1/2" Bottom
3 1/4" Middle
2 5/8" Top
1/8"
1/2"
3/8"
10 5/8"
1/8"
1/4"

[25] CUT THE TONGUE ON THE DRAWER FRONT
While the backs should fit right into their dadoes, the fronts need a 1/8"-thick (3mm) tongue cut on either end. Cut these tongues by running the pieces past the blade on end. Clamp a scrap to the pieces that run along the top of the fence for added support. Adjust the fence to control the thickness of the tongues.

[26] CUT THE SLOT FOR THE DRAWER BOTTOM
Tilt the blade to match the slot on the drawer sides. Position the rip fence to cut the slots in the side for the drawer bottom. Straighten the blade. Transfer the location of the slots to the drawer fronts and backs. Cut these slots as well.

[27] SCREW THE DRAWERS TOGETHER
Because of the angles involved, it is difficult to simply clamp the drawers together. Instead, I use screws. Counterbore and drill holes for the screws. Apply glue, then screw the pieces together.

[28] ATTACH THE DRAWER FACES
Sand the front face of the drawer box flat. Tape a fresh sheet of sandpaper to the saw table, then scrub the drawer boxes across it. Working this way makes everything flush and keeps the whole surface flat.
Cut the drawer faces to size and glue them to the drawer boxes. Sand everything flush. Stain and finish the case and drawers. Paint the legs. Finally, install the pulls on the drawers.

[SUPPLIERS]

ADAMS & KENNEDY — THE WOOD SOURCE
6178 Mitch Owen Rd.
P.O. Box 700
Manotick, ON
Canada K4M 1A6
613-822-6800
www.wood-source.com
Wood supply

ADJUSTABLE CLAMP COMPANY
404 N. Armour St.
Chicago, IL 60622
312-666-0640
www.adjustableclamp.com
Clamps and woodworking tools

B&Q
B&Q
Portswood House
1 Hampshire Corporate Park
Chandlers Ford
Eastleigh
Hampshire, England SO53 3YX
0845 609 6688
www.diy.com
Woodworking tools, supplies and hardware

BIESEMEYER MANUFACTURING
216 South Alma School Road, Suite 3
Mesa, Arizona 85210
800-782-1831
www.biesemeyer.com
fences, guards, splitters

BUSY BEE TOOLS
130 Great Gulf Dr.
Concord, ON
Canada L4K 5W1
1-800-461-2879
www.busybeetools.com
Woodworking tools and supplies

CMT USA INC
307-F Pomona Drive
Greensboro, North Carolina 27407
888-268-2487
wwwcmtusa.com
cove cutter, carbide-tipped tooling

CONSTANTINE'S WOOD CENTER OF FLORIDA
1040 E. Oakland Park Blvd.
Fort Lauderdale, FL 33334
800-443-9667
www.constantines.com
Tools, woods, veneers, hardware

FRANK PAXTON LUMBER COMPANY
5701 W. Sixty-sixth St.
Chicago, IL 60638
800-323-2203
www.paxtonwood.com
Wood, hardware, tools, books

FORREST MANUFACTURING
461 River Road
Clifton, New Jersey 07014
800-733-7111
forrest.woodmall.com
blades, dado sets, sharpening

FREUD TOOLS
218 Feld Avenue
High Point, North Carolina 27263
800-334-4107
www.freudtools.com
blades, dado sets, box joint cutter

THE HOME DEPOT
2455 Paces Ferry Rd.
Atlanta, GA 30339
800-553-3199 (U.S.)
800-628-0525 (Canada)
www.homedepot.com
Woodworking tools, supplies and hardware

LRH ENTERPRISES
9250 Independence Avenue
Chatsworth, California 91311
800-423-2544
www.lrhent.com
Magic Molder

LEE VALLEY TOOLS LTD.
P.O. Box 1780
Ogdensburg, NY 13669-6780
800-871-8158 (U.S.)
800-267-8767 (Canada)
www.leevalley.com
Woodworking tools and hardware

LOWE'S
P.O. Box 1111
North Wilkesboro, NC 28656
800-445-6937
www.lowes.com
Woodworking tools, supplies and hardware

ROCKLER WOODWORKING AND HARDWARE
4365 Willow Dr.
Medina, MN 55340
800-279-4441
www.rockler.com
Woodworking tools, hardware and books

TOOL TREND LTD.
140 Snow Blvd.
Thornhill, ON
Canada L4K 4L1
416-663-8665
Woodworking tools and hardware

TREND MACHINERY & CUTTING TOOLS LTD.
Odhams Trading Estate
St. Albans Rd.
Watford
Hertfordshire, U.K.
WD24 7TR
01923 224657
www.trendmachinery.co.uk
Woodworking tools and hardware

VAUGHAN & BUSHNELL MFG. CO.
11414 Maple Ave.
Hebron, IL 60034
815-648-2446
www.vaughanmfg.com
Hammers and other tools

WINDY RIDGE WOODWORKS
6751 Hollenbach Rd.
New Tripoli, Pennsylvania 18066
610 767-4515
www.wrwoodworks.com
fine furniture and cabinetry, woodworking instruction, woodworking books

WOODCRAFT SUPPLY CORP.
1177 Rosemar Rd.
P.O. Box 1686
Parkersburg, WV 26102
800-535-4482
www.woodcraft.com
Woodworking hardware

WOODWORKER'S HARDWARE
P.O. Box 180
Sauk Rapids, MN 56379-0180
800-383-0130
www.wwhardware.com
Woodworking hardware

WOODWORKER'S SUPPLY
1108 N. Glenn Rd.
Casper, WY 82601
800-645-9292
http://woodworker.com
Woodworking tools and accessories, finishing supplies, books and plans

[INDEX]

MORE GREAT TITLES FROM POPULAR WOODWORKING!

GLEN HUEY'S ILLUSTRATED GUIDE TO BUILDING PERIOD FURNITURE

By Glen Huey

Woodworkers will learn to build their own high-end period furniture with clear, concise instructions, step-by-step photos and a bonus DVD ROM of real-time demonstrations and printable plans.

ISBN 13: 978-1-55870-770-2
ISBN 10: 1-55870-770-0, pb, 128 p, #70722

POPULAR WOODWORKING POCKET SHOP REFERENCE

By Tom Begnal

Woodworkers will find concise and accurate information about a broad range of woodworking topics, covering everything from furniture design and materials to adhesives, tools, safety and more. Lay flat binding and handy pocket size make this easy-to-reference guide the perfect resource for any woodshop.

ISBN 13: 978-1-55870-782-5
ISBN 10: 1-55870-782-4
hc w/ concealed wire-o, 240 p., # Z0227

THE COMPLETE CABINETMAKER'S REFERENCE

By Jeffrey Piontkowski

This indispensable resource for cabinetmakers includes cutting and assembly instructions, along with lists of types and quantities of materials needed for all standard-sized cabinets. You'll also learn how to adapt the projects to build custom-sized pieces.

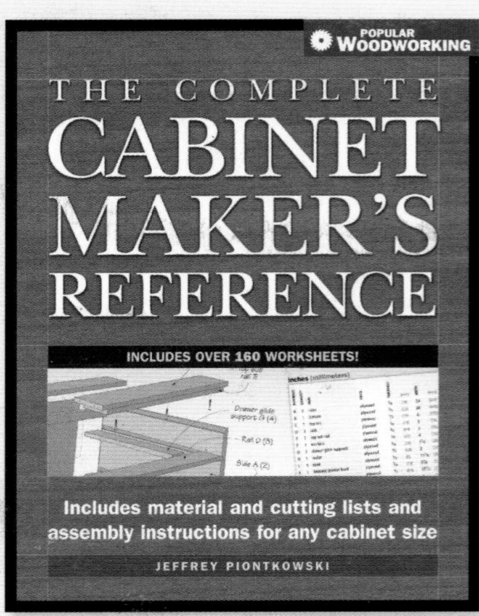

ISBN 13: 978-1-55870-757-3
ISBN 10: 1-55870-757-3, pb, 128 p, #70710

POPULAR WOODWORKING PRACTICAL SHOP MATH

By Tom Begnal

Portable and easy-to-use, this handy guide makes the perfect comprehensive "cheat sheet" to woodworking math. It explains math formulas and conversions in simple layman's terms, and includes sections on working with fractions and decimals, dimensioned drawings and more.

ISBN 13: 978-1-55870-783-2
ISBN 10: 1-55870-783-2
hc w/ concealed wire-o, 240 p., # Z0226

THESE AND OTHER GREAT WOODWORKING BOOKS ARE AVAILABLE AT YOUR LOCAL BOOKSTORE, WOODWORKING STORES, OR FROM ONLINE SUPPLIERS.

www.popularwoodworking.com